CONTENTS

ACKNOWLEDGEMENTS

We would like to express our thanks to the Local Government Association for sponsoring this research project, and to Julia Bennett, Kirsten Liddell, David Bruce, Marilyn Cohen, Margaret Lochrie and Sue Owen for their support and helpful comments on the draft report.

We are most grateful to all our interviewees for taking time to share their views and experiences of early education and childcare services with us.

We would also like to express our gratitude to the following people at NFER: Judy Bradley, Valerie Gee, Jo Richards, David Pye and Laura Sukhnandan for their comments on drafts of the report, and Alison Bannerman, Louise Brennan and Laura Duckett for their administrative support. Thanks also to Mary Hargreaves and Rose James for their Desk Top Publishing support. Finally, we are most grateful to Monika Wray and David Upton for their editorial contribution.

EXECUTIVE SUMMARY

Background

The Labour Government launched its National Childcare Strategy in 1998. The Strategy confirmed the Government's commitment to promoting better childcare. This, it was felt, could be achieved through the better integration of education and childcare services to ensure childcare that was of high quality, affordable and accessible. The Strategy provided the framework within which the Government would work with local authorities. The authorities themselves were to take the lead and work in close partnership with local stakeholders, such as providers, parents and others.

Earlier research by the National Children's Bureau (McQuail and Pugh, 1995) had identified three main organisational models for the management of early years and childcare services in local authorities – integrated, coordinated and collaborative. The NFER study picked up and developed these models in order to follow up and extend the previous work in this field.

Aims and objectives

This study formed part of the Local Government Association's Educational Research Programme. It was designed to investigate which strategies had been agreed by local authorities for the organisation of their services for children under five in England and Wales. It set out to examine which authorities had adopted which of the three models of organisation outlined above; to describe examples of good practice and to highlight the advantages and disadvantages of different models.

Methodology

The research was in two phases. Phase One was a familiarisation with the main strategies adopted by local authorities. This was done through a questionnaire survey sent to all local authorities in England and Wales. Phase Two involved detailed case studies of eight quite different local authorities using different organisational models. In this second phase, the intention was to understand how the chosen organisational model had been arrived at, how it had developed and how it was now working. Two researcher days were spent in each of the case study authorities and discussions were held with elected representatives, officers, providers and their representatives. This report draws on both phases of the research, which was carried out between May 1999 and February 2000.

Key findings

The survey achieved a very high response rate of 93 per cent. The majority of local authorities which responded had adopted a **coordinated** model for organising their early years service. This meant that, while there were still essentially separate departments and services within the authority, they worked together, within a formalised structure, on early years issues. In many authorities, the council members and department directors shared a vision of coordination and supported the structural arrangements for the early years service. The Early Years Coordinator maintained close links with senior officers and with other partners. This type of organisation was most common in the counties, outer London boroughs, and in the new unitary authorities.

The **integrated** model, where a single department or service was responsible for early years matters, was in use in 17 per cent of the authorities. This model was more common (though not exclusively so) in inner London and metropolitan boroughs, where there was a denser population and the area covered by the authority was relatively compact. It was usual in these authorities for the Early Years Development and Childcare Partnership (EYDCP) to be fully integrated into the organisational structure of the authority as one of a number of strategy or working groups.

The **collaborative** model, where officers continued to work in quite separate departments, was in use in 14 per cent of authorities. In these cases, there were clear lines of demarcation between departments and it was up to the Early Years Coordinator to liaise with officers and partners. The model was not associated with any particular type of authority.

There was some indication from the study that half of those authorities which now had a collaborative model in place were moving towards greater coordination and that many of those which were now using a coordinated approach were considering moving towards greater integration. An analysis of the EYDCP Plans suggested that there was some relationship between the choice of strategy adopted and a number of factors, including: type of authority (i.e. county, unitary, inner or outer London or metropolitan); geography; demography; economy; employment patterns; population mix and needs; and history.

A combination of factors had usually influenced an authority's choice of organisational model or the model that had been allowed to evolve. In addition to those factors mentioned above, the following also mattered: existing working practices, the impact of national initiatives, local government reorganisation, and the political composition of the council. How far the local authority itself provided and managed most of the early years provision was also important, as was the size of the under-fives population.

The detailed case studies showed that integrated, coordinated or collaborative structures were differently interpreted in different locations. The models chosen were designed to suit local circumstances. For example, integration could mean slightly different things in different authorities, depending on their local circumstances.

Local authorities had arrived at their preferred organisational model through a number of routes. Some had started planning for integrated services as far back as 1989 when the Children Act (GB. Statutes, 1989) was passed. In some authorities, there were examples of committed senior officers who had shared a vision of integration or coordination and who had worked long and hard to achieve it. Other authorities had taken the opportunity provided by local government reorganisation to take a fresh look at their services. Yet others had been spurred on by the National Childcare Strategy itself.

Undoubtedly, those authorities that achieved most integration or coordination were much aided by a shared vision, commitment and support from the top, a willingness by officers to work across department boundaries and a good relationship between the authority and the Partnership.

The more integrated or coordinated the early years service was, the more streamlined and focused the provision was seen to be. Where there was a discrete Early Years Unit and a designated coordinator and where structured opportunities existed for a dedicated team to plan strategically together on early years issues, inter-departmental tensions seemed to be absent, duplication was avoided and a more coherent service was seen to be delivered. Both providers and end users benefited as they were given visible and accessible opportunities to communicate and contribute.

In authorities operating a collaborative approach, there was potential for less strategic planning, a greater risk of inefficiency and duplication, less responsiveness to early education and childcare needs and the possible professional and actual isolation of the Early Years Coordinator. This model sits less well with the demands of the National Childcare Strategy.

This study would have to conclude that, while it is too early to see how well authorities are delivering their services as most are still in their infancy, there need to be different models available to meet local needs. While collaboration is certainly not ideal, integration need not be the goal to which all authorities should work even though it is the perfect solution for some. Coordination is a totally appropriate response to the organisation of early education and childcare services in many contexts.

1. INTRODUCTION

The Labour Government launched its National Childcare Strategy in 1998. The Strategy confirmed the Government's commitment to promoting better childcare, which, it felt, could be achieved through better integration of education and childcare services.

This research study formed part of the Local Government Association's Educational Research Programme and began in April 1999. Its intention was to follow up and extend previous research on the organisation by local authorities of childcare and early education services in England and Wales. Its main aim was to explore and examine which organisational models were being used by authorities to structure their services, to understand how the structures had evolved and been developed and to identify the main advantages and disadvantages of different models.

This report provides an overview of the main types of strategy which have been adopted to bring about the coordination of early education and childcare services. It presents a national picture of the numbers of authorities using different approaches and then offers some more detailed examples, through eight case studies, of practices in different authorities. The case studies examine how their current service came about, how it is run and what implications this has had for officers, providers and parents.

2. BACKGROUND

The Government has stated its commitment to making life better for people. It wants to deliver 'responsive public services' – a commitment restated in one of its most recent White Papers. In *Modernising Government* (GB. Parliament. HoC, 1999), the Prime Minister and the Cabinet pledged to deliver public services through 'a big push on obstacles to joined-up working, through local partnerships, one-stop shops, and other means... [These services would] involve and meet the needs of different groups in society' (p. 7). A number of new initiatives over the last few years have called for the cooperation of different departments and organisations, for example the regeneration of local communities, one-stop shops for public services, Education Action Zones, to name but three.

Early years education and childcare is an area where the Government would like to see greater integration between planners, regulators and providers to deliver a better service. While it is agreed by the Government that parents should decide what sort of childcare they want for their children, the Government sees it as its responsibility to ensure that parents have access to services to enable them to make genuine choices.

There is currently a variety of provision for children under five in England and Wales. The main ones are: early admission into primary school reception classes; playgroups; local authority day nurseries; family centres; private nurseries; nursery schools; nursery classes in primary schools; and childminders. And, within each of these broad categories, there is a wide range of different services offering various degrees of early education and/ or daycare. This provision is coordinated to a greater or lesser degree in different local authorities.

In its National Childcare Strategy, announced in May 1998, the Government acknowledged that an increasing proportion of mothers (many of them lone parents) were now working outside the home and that not all could or did rely on informal sources, such as friends or family members, for the care of their children. The Government restated its commitment to supporting families and children by 'promoting the well-being of children, offering equal opportunities for parents, especially women, and to supporting parents in balancing work and family life' (GB. DfEE, 1998, p. 6). The Strategy announced plans to ensure good-quality, affordable childcare for children aged 0 to 14 in every neighbourhood, including both formal childcare and support arrangements. Raising the quality of care would 'include better integration of early education and childcare' (GB. DfEE, 1998, p. 6).

The Strategy described childcare services in the UK as having three key problems: the quality of childcare can be variable; the cost of care is high and out of reach of many parents; and in some areas, there are not enough childcare places and/or parents' access to them is hampered by poor information.

Several promises formed part of this Strategy: the creation of more opportunities for childcare training through the New Deal; a new childcare tax credit for working families (Working Families Tax Credit); more and varied childcare places to meet parents' preferences; the opportunity for every four-year-old to be given the chance of a free education place and, in the longer term, extending similar opportunities to three-year-olds; and new childcare partnerships based on the existing Early Years Development Partnerships.

The success of the Government's approach would be tested through better outcomes for children and by more parents having the chance (if they so wished) to take up work, education or training as a result. The successful outcomes of the Strategy would also depend on the commitment of and cooperation between local authorities and a wide range of partners – providers in the private and voluntary sectors, employers, Training and Enterprise Councils (TECs), colleges, schools, health authorities, church authorities, special educational needs groups and parents, all of whom have local knowledge and expertise. Local authorities are key partners in the Government's plans.

The Government's 1998 commitment to improved childcare provision was preceded by several national initiatives stretching back over several decades. There had been a steadily growing demand for facilities for young children for many years. In 1972, the Government White Paper *Education: Framework for Expansion* (GB. Parliament. HoC, 1972) recognised that learning opportunities for young children needed to be provided by many agencies with a variety of experience and skills to contribute. One type of provision would not meet all needs. It was appreciated that there would always be competition for limited resources and that these needed therefore to be targeted more effectively. It recommended the provision of nursery education for 50 per cent of three-year-olds and 90 per cent of four-year-olds, but cuts in Government spending meant that this vision was not put into practice.

The Children Act of 1989 (GB. Statutes, 1989) stated that local authorities had principal responsibility for coordinating and providing services for children in need. It encouraged local authority departments to work together and cooperate across their boundaries in order to provide, regulate and review day care services for children in their area.

The Act gave local authorities the duty to:

- provide day care services for children in need;
- regulate the private and voluntary day care sectors and childminders;
- publish information about services provided by themselves and others;
- encourage Social Services and Education Departments to jointly conduct and publish a report of their day care provision every three years.

When the Audit Commission published its study of education for under-fives, *Counting to Five* (Audit Commission, 1996 and 1997), provision for children of this age was largely left to the discretion of individual local authorities. The services available varied from one authority to another, depending on the policies of the authority and initiatives taken by voluntary and private sector providers.

Counting to Five set out three major issues for local authorities to address:

- access to services was uneven, varying from one authority to another and from place to place within an authority;

- the educational quality of individual settings (schools, playgroups, private nurseries, etc) varied, although all types of provider could do well; and

- costs were variable, both within and between different types of setting, with no evidence of a link between quality and cost. The key factors affecting costs were found to be staff pay and levels of occupancy.

The Audit Commission stressed the importance of focusing on the needs of parents and children, and of meeting those needs through a mix of provision. Local authorities were urged to work with providers in the voluntary and private sectors to ensure a more streamlined approach to services for children under five. Local authorities were to think strategically, work with others, secure appropriate provision, involve parents, focus on quality, use resources efficiently and see planning as part of a long-term process.

Keen to encourage more early years education, the Conservative Government introduced a voucher scheme in April 1996 (pilot) and April 1997 (nationwide) entitling all four-year-olds to part-time education for the three terms before they were required to start school at the age of five. Following the general election in May 1997, the new Labour Government announced its intention to replace the voucher system with a planned system of provision for the under-fives. It was still fully committed to offering some provision for all four-year-olds.

This new approach to education and care for the under-fives, enshrined in the National Childcare Strategy, was based on the principle of partnership between local authorities and private and voluntary providers. In 1997, all local authorities set up Early Years Development Partnerships. These Partnerships were created to involve all providers, services, agencies and stakeholders in the field. Their mission was to facilitate the planning and delivery of services for children under five.

Each Partnership had to draw up an Early Years Development Plan based on joint discussions, and the local authority was to be responsible for its implementation. The Partnerships and their Plans were to ensure that:

- early years services were planned by a representative body at local level;

- historical traditions, demographic changes and socio-economic characteristics were taken into account.

There was a need, therefore, to review current provision, identify gaps and plan to meet them, identify services wanted by parents, agree minimum training and qualifications requirements and provide support and training to staff working in all areas.

In 1998, on publication of *Meeting the Childcare Challenge* (GB. DfEE, 1998), the Government expanded the remit of the Early Years Development Partnerships so that they became Early Years Development and Childcare Partnerships (EYDCPs). This applied throughout England, whereas arrangements for Wales were still to be put into place. The main targets of the EYDCPs, as spelled out in the DfEE Guidance document are to: 'provide a good quality, free early education place for all four-year-olds whose parents want one...and for an agreed percentage of three-year-olds by 2001–2...and good quality, affordable childcare for children aged 0–14 in every neighbourhood' (GB. DfEE, 1999a, para. 1.6).

To encourage the development of services, a number of Early Excellence Centres have been and will be set up throughout the country to provide models of good quality practice for local childcare providers. The centres are designed to bring together facilities for education and care and thereby to ensure better support for parents and carers, a more consistent regulatory regime, new standards for early education and childcare and a framework for staff training.

Funding for these new initiatives has come in part directly from central government and in part from grants and bids from the Standards Fund, the DfEE, the National Lottery New Opportunities Fund (NOF), the European Social Fund and the Single Regeneration Budget (SRB).

In 1999, the Government put aside some £450 million for the next three years to provide for 250 Sure Start projects in areas of greatest need in England. These are projects aimed specifically at families with children under the age of four. Sure Start has been described, by its Head of Unit, as 'a radical cross-departmental strategy to improve services for young children and families' (Eisenstadt, 1999). Its main aims are 'to prevent social exclusion, raise educational performance and reduce health inequalities' (op. cit.). Sure Start projects will provide a range of services for local families, including

- advice and support;
- play facilities and educational provision to involve parents;
- primary health care services;
- good-quality childcare provision;
- outreach workers to provide support in the home for parents.

The projects will develop from and build on existing local provision. The idea is to reach some 100,000 children, aged 0–three years by building on best practice and existing services to provide 'an integrated approach which will encompass the factors which research, both in this country and overseas, has proved work best for young children and their families' (LGA, 1998).

Speaking in Parliament in June 1999, the Employment and Equal Opportunities Minister summed up progress at that time:

- four out of five young children were getting their early years experience in nursery school, nursery classes or reception classes;

- a total of 66,000 new childcare places had been created in England in the first year since the launch of the Government's National Childcare Strategy;

- 17 Early Excellence Centres were up and running;

- 21 Sure Start trailblazer projects had received the go-ahead to establish programmes later in 1999;

- the Qualifications and Curriculum Authority was leading the initiative to build a qualifications and training framework for the childcare sector;

- the TECs had received £11million to provide more childcare training and business support;

- almost all Partnerships had signed up to the Childcare Information Systems Development project linking local databases to a national website holding core childcare information (GB. DfEE, 1999b).

At the point when the fieldwork began in the current NFER study (June 1999), local authorities were still developing and/or refining their strategies and structures for early years provision. They were assessing and addressing the quantity and quality of available provision, exploring further what the needs were in their localities, putting Government initiatives into place and determining how best to deliver a service that took account of existing stakeholders and allowed them to be involved in strategic planning. How far the attention and resources devoted to early childhood services since the Labour Government came into office in 1997 had resulted in a coherent service had yet to be seen.

3. RESEARCH METHODOLOGY

In the spring of 1999, the NFER was commissioned by the Local Government Association (LGA), as part of its educational research programme, to follow up and extend previous research into the organisation of childcare and education services for the under-fives in England and Wales.

3.1 Previous research and developments

Probably the most significant study in recent years on the organisation of early childhood services was that carried out by the National Children's Bureau (NCB) (McQuail and Pugh, 1995). The main aim of their study was 'to assess the extent to which changes in the way in which early childhood services were organised had resulted in improvements (in quantity and quality) to services for young children and their families' (p. 1). The hypothesis was 'that at any given level of resources, working together across departments and other agencies provides better value for money, whether as better quality and more flexible services, or as more services' (p. 1). The study also sought to explore whether 'working together' was better achieved through three different models of organisation:

- ◆ 'integration' – where there were 'unified under fives services, with a committee or sub-committee of the council with substantial delegated authority'

- ◆ 'coordination' – where there were 'significant formal arrangements between departments at member and officer level'

- ◆ 'collaboration' – where there were 'few formal arrangements beyond the ordinary corporate management arrangements of the authority'.

The NCB study consisted of case studies of 11 English local authorities. It concluded that all the authorities, '...whatever their organisational arrangements, were attempting to bring coherence, clarity of purpose and increased public attention to services for young children' (p. 8). The authorities argued that they had done this 'in spite of a lack of a clear lead and coordinated action from the two central government Departments most closely involved – the Department of Education and Department of Health' (p. 8). Different organisational structures tended to reflect different traditions – political, demographic and historical – and what was provided depended on these.

The NCB study showed that authorities which had adopted integrated arrangements tended to be those in inner London and metropolitan areas, which provided high levels of day care provision and which shared a commitment to addressing issues of poverty and equal opportunities.

'Coordinated' and 'collaborative' arrangements were more often to be found in the counties and outer London boroughs. They depended more on the private and voluntary sectors for provision and had a high commitment to involving and supporting parents.

The study finally concluded that: 'If the aim is for universal services offering care and education to all children whose parents want it, then an "integrated" approach appears to be most effective. However, if a mixed economy of services is to continue, the relationships between the local authority and the voluntary and private sectors will need attention in some authorities' (p. 9). Different structures of organisation were found to have their advantages. The more coherent the approach, however, the more visible were the advantages for children, families, providers and local authorities alike.

The NCB study summed up by stating that: 'The key is to develop strategies for planning, resourcing and reviewing high quality services for young children that are "*owned*" by all elected members and senior officers. These strategies need to be supported by the capacity to make executive decisions, which requires some control over budgets. An overall vision, shared by all "*stakeholders*" and which takes account of local circumstances and traditions, together with the means of implementing it, is as important as the type of political or management structure' (p. 9).

In the years since the NCB reported its findings, Early Years Development Partnerships, later to be called Early Years Development and Childcare Partnerships (EYDCPs), representing all the early years interests in the area, have been established in each local authority to help plan early years services.

Each Partnership is obliged to produce an Early Years Development Plan. In 1998–99, the Plan needed, as a minimum, to show how the local authority would secure three free terms of good-quality pre-school education for all four-year-olds, including those with special educational needs, prior to them becoming of compulsory school age, whose parents wanted it. Plans also needed to demonstrate how cooperation and collaboration between local authorities and the private and voluntary sectors could be used to secure these places and how places would be matched to the needs of children and their parents. Plans had to show how Partnerships were addressing the strategic principles of the National Childcare Strategy. The 1999–2000 Plans were to build on earlier ones and show progress. See Jamieson and Owen (2000) for a comprehensive account of the development and role of Early Years Development and Childcare Partnerships.

3.2 The research brief, methodology and sample

The main aim of the NFER study was to investigate what strategies had been devised for the organisation of services for children under five. It set out to examine Early Years Development Plans of local authorities from across England so as to identify the range of organisational strategies which had been adopted; to see how the Plans had been implemented; to demonstrate examples of good practice and to highlight the advantages and disadvantages of different models in different local contexts.

The research was in two phases:

♦ Phase One – a familiarisation with the main strategies adopted by local authorities for the coordination of services for under-fives as detailed in EYDCP Plans.

♦ Phase Two – a detailed study of the early years service in eight local authorities, focusing on their evolution, aims and objectives, implementation, monitoring and evaluation, successes and challenges and any modifications made to their original EYDCP Plans.

Phase One involved a questionnaire survey of all the 172 local authorities in England and Wales to ascertain which organisational model they were using to deliver their early years and childcare service.

Phase Two was based on eight case studies of authorities each using one of the three different organisational models. A researcher spent two days in each authority interviewing local authority officers, elected representatives, providers and their representatives. A total of 44 interviews were conducted: 19 with local authority officers including planning officers, Assistant Chief Education Officers, Directors and Early Years Officers; 14 with early education and childcare providers of whom nine were members of an EYDCP; seven with chairs of EYDCPs and four with elected members of councils.

The resulting information was subjected to detailed analysis to establish what each authority had decided to do, why and with what effect. All case study descriptions were returned to the local authorities and redrafted in the light of their comments.

The study was carried out between May 1999 and February 2000.

Notes

- Some of the statistical data returned by the local authorities with their Plans referred to 1991 census data. Since then, some local authorities have undergone reorganisation and therefore the figures quoted may not, at times, reflect current authority boundaries and may not, therefore, be fully accurate.

- Many local authorities, in providing figures for their under-fives population, gave statistics which included all children aged 0–5. Local authorities are only obliged to provide early education and childcare places for four years olds and above and some three-year-olds.

- After the NFER visits to the eight local authorities were completed, the case studies were drafted and sent back to the authorities for correction and approval. Some of the structures in place were complex and it was important that the NFER represented an accurate picture.

- In the sections that follow, the acronym EYDCP or the word Partnership is used to refer to the Early Years Development and Childcare Partnerships. The plans they are required to submit to the DfEE are referred to either as Plans or EYDCP Plans.

4. OVERVIEW OF THE MAIN FINDINGS

4.1 Phase One – the national picture

The research team developed a pro forma (see Appendix 1) which was sent to the early years representative in each of the 172 local authorities in England and Wales in June 1999. (The small islands authorities of Jersey, Guernsey, the Isles of Scilly and the Isle of Man were not included in the study as they are not required to set up Partnerships and prepare Early Years Development and Childcare Plans.)

The pro forma described three organisational models for the structure of childcare and education services for children under five. Local authority early years representatives were asked to indicate which strategy best reflected their service and practice. The three organisational models were based on those identified by the National Children's Bureau in 1995, but were further refined after consultation with NFER's Education Management Information Exchange (EMIE) service and with the Local Government Association's (LGA) lead officer for childcare and early years. Each local authority was also asked to submit a copy of its Early Years Development and Childcare Plan to the NFER.

The three models of organisation – as defined on the pro forma – were as follows:

A) 'essentially a single department/service' (integrated);

B) 'essentially separate departments/services which collaborate within a formal structure' (coordinated);

C) 'essentially separate departments/services' (collaborative).

The response from the local authorities was very high – 160 (93 per cent) returned the pro forma; only 12 did not respond. Proportionately fewer responses were received from Welsh authorities (14 out of 22). This lower response rate from the Welsh authorities can be accounted for in part by the fact that significant changes were going on in the Welsh Assembly at the time when the pro forma was dispatched, and, in part, by the fact that some Welsh local authorities were sharing services and therefore a non-response from one person could result in no information from several authorities. A total of 98 (57 per cent of all authorities) also provided their Plans.

The table overleaf shows that the *coordinated* model was by far the most popular: the majority (106 or 62 per cent) of local authorities had adopted this approach. Of the rest, 30 (17 per cent) had adopted the *integrated* model and 24 (14 per cent) had opted for the *collaborative* structure.

Numbers and percentages of local authorities adopting different organisational models of early years and childcare service

Type of local authority	Integrated model	Coordinated model	Collaborative model	Total responses	No response
Inner London (13)	8	3	1	12	1
Outer London (20)	2	14	2	18	2
Metropolitan (36)	11	19	5	35	1
Welsh (22)	1	9	4	14	8
New unitary (47)	3	35	9	47	0
County (34)	5	26	3	34	0
TOTAL = 172 100%	30 17%	106 62%	24 14%	160 93%	12 7%

From the comments added to the pro formas, there was some indication that at least half of those authorities which now had a collaborative approach were moving towards greater coordination and that many of the authorities now using a coordinated approach were developing it to become more integrated. It is important to note, however, that not all authorities aspired to have totally integrated services. Some felt that coordination enabled them to respond best and most flexibly to the needs of their end users.

More detailed analysis of the pro forma returns and the EYDCP Plans suggested that there was a relationship between the choice of strategy and a number of other factors:

- type of authority (i.e. county/unitary/inner or outer London/ metropolitan);

- geographical composition and spread (i.e. urban/rural, size, supply/demand for services);

- demography (i.e. affluent/deprived, proportion of under-fives, ethnic mix, population mobility);

- economy and employment history;

- infrastructure (ease of transport etc); and

- local authority history (reorganisation, established working practices and philosophy).

These relationships are discussed in more detail in the rest of this chapter.

The integrated model

A total of 30 authorities had adopted an integrated model (i.e. 'essentially a single department/service') for organising and servicing their early years provision. For the most part, they tended to be authorities located in small, densely populated urban areas with a high level of socio-economic deprivation.

Most inner London boroughs (eight out of 13) and almost a third of all metropolitan boroughs had well-established integrated structures, identifiable at all levels in the authority. This usually meant that there was a team of designated officers responsible for service delivery, based either in a discrete Early Years Unit or in a section within an established council department, usually the Education Department.

In the authorities operating an integrated model, it was usual for the Partnership to be fully integrated into the organisational structure of the authority as one of a number of strategy or working groups. Such strategy groups, designed to ensure that local interests were represented in authority policy and planning, had often existed in these authorities for many years. The EYDCP involvement was mainly consultative, as the local authority retained executive decision-making powers.

Typically, the main early years provider in authorities with integrated arrangements was the local authority itself. The authority also tended to hold a strong control over maintained provision and over plans for expansion or development. The voluntary and private sector providers in these authorities, while part of the EYDCP, were sometimes represented in smaller proportions than suggested in the DfEE guidance.

As many of the authorities with integrated approaches were in urban areas, it is perhaps not surprising that the majority were also involved in a range of central government initiatives aimed at tackling urban degeneration, social exclusion and deprivation. These authorities were probably also in a better position to build these initiatives into their early years strategies. Those most commonly cited included Education Action Zones, Sure Start Initiatives, Early Excellence Centres, New Deal Partnerships and New Opportunities Fund.

The coordinated model

The coordinated model was by far the most common model in use. This was defined as 'essentially separate departments/services which collaborate within a formal structure'. This model was more often operating in the counties, the outer London boroughs and in the new unitary authorities. A total of 106 local authorities that responded (or 62 per cent of all authorities) were using this approach.

While the authorities using a coordinated model varied considerably in size, most had quite discrete rural and urban areas, stable employment patterns and well-developed infrastructures. All, however, were also able to identify significant pockets of deprivation in their authorities in rural areas where agriculture provided the major source of employment and/or in urban areas where there had been a decline in manufacturing and heavy industries. The more deprived communities within these authorities tended to use early years provision maintained by the local authority, whereas the more affluent communities tended to use voluntary and private sector provision.

Coordination in rural authorities usually meant that a number of smaller groups, such as district and local forums, parish councils or satellite partnerships, met at local level and then worked together at 'central' meetings – such as ones involving all Partnership representatives. This ensured that local representatives came together both to share local issues and to address the wider needs of the entire authority.

In many authorities, the council members and departmental directors shared a vision of coordination and supported the structural arrangements for the early years service. Even though there were separate departments for Social Services and Education in these authorities, the majority had a nominated officer to coordinate all early years issues, to service the Partnership and to be a conduit for contact and for the sharing of good practice. This officer was usually based in the Education Department but s/he maintained close links with senior officers in other departments and with under-eights workers in Social Services as well as with other partner organisations.

Even though in most of the authorities with a coordinated approach, the Partnership sat on the periphery of the local authority structure, it was welcomed as an opportunity to develop ties across local authority departments and with the voluntary and private sectors, to influence policy and to plan strategically. These authorities tended to view the National Childcare Strategy as a valued opportunity to encourage closer working relationships and to share good practice.

Authorities with coordinated services were often eligible to bid for some central government initiatives, for example, Early Excellence Centres, especially for their more deprived areas. Most felt, however, that they did not attract sufficient national funding of this kind because of the relative affluence of some other communities in their area.

The collaborative model

The collaborative approach (i.e. 'essentially separate departments/services') to early years services was only being used by 24 of the authorities which responded. It is worth noting that half of these suggested that they were moving towards greater coordination. No particular type of authority was especially associated with the collaborative model.

In these authorities, there were clear lines of demarcation between departments. Generally, a designated Early Years Officer, whose duties were to service the Partnership and to liaise and exchange information with officers in other departments, had been appointed to the Education Department. S/he tended to be the main point of contact for providers.

From information included in the Partnership Plans and from notes made on the pro formas returned to the NFER, the EYDCP appeared to have quite a low status within these authorities.

4.2 Phase Two – profile of the case study authorities

Eight authorities were selected as case study candidates. The eight were chosen to represent a range of different types of local authority and the range of organisational models adopted. The case studies themselves appear in full in the next section of this report, but here we examine the main findings to have emerged from Phase Two of the research.

Of the eight local authorities studied, four were identified as using an integrated model. One of these was in the process of moving from a coordinated to an integrated structure at the time of the research, but was included as an example of an integrated model. Two authorities were working with a coordinated model and another two were using a collaborative one. Six were happy to be identified; two preferred to remain anonymous and so they have been given a pseudonym. The characteristics of the selected authorities are outlined below.

Examples of the integrated model

- ◆ Hampshire – a large, mainly rural county with a number of urban conurbations. The area as a whole is considered to be quite affluent. The authority had a long-established integrated structure.

- ◆ Camden – a small, densely populated inner London borough with a diverse socio-economic and ethnic mix and a well-established integrated approach to early years services.

- ◆ York – a new unitary authority, geographically small and predominantly urban. This authority was moving from a coordinated to a more integrated approach at the time of the research.

- ◆ Slough – a new unitary authority, densely populated and urban, and with a substantial percentage of families from ethnic minority backgrounds. Slough had recently reorganised its structure to coincide with local authority reorganisation.

Examples of the coordinated model

- ◆ Powys – a large unitary authority in Wales, sparsely populated, with a few small, dispersed towns and a predominantly rural community. Transport in the rural areas is not easy.

- ◆ Wakefield – a metropolitan borough, made up equally of rural and urban areas.

Examples of the collaborative model

♦ Southlea (pseudonym) – a well-established borough in the south east of England, with pockets of deprivation and some of affluence. This authority has plans to move towards a more coordinated structure in the future.

♦ Fulsham (pseudonym) – a recently formed unitary authority, covering both urban and rural areas, considered to be affluent overall.

4.3 Main findings to emerge from the case studies

> A combination of factors had influenced an authority's choice of organisational model. While an integrated model was very efficient for some authorities, it was not considered appropriate for others. An integrated model was not the goal for all.

Several factors affected why the local authorities had chosen a particular organisational model for their early years service. Most often, it was a model that had evolved and/or been developed from already established working practices and patterns of provision. These practices were also often influenced by the authority's history and geography, the political composition of the council and its response to the National Childcare Strategy and to previous national initiatives on early years. A combination of these factors was most usually at play.

Even though most of the authorities described their current models of organisation as still developing and evolving and, therefore, open to change, the models in use at the time of the research were usually the result of **existing practice**. Integrated and coordinated models were more common in authorities where officers were used – to a greater or lesser extent – to working across departmental boundaries and where there was commitment and support from the very top to corporate working. Collaborative models, on the other hand, were more the norm where departmental delineation was still the main working practice within the authority as a whole.

While the four authorities that had an integrated model in place were different politically (three were Labour-led and one Conservative-led) and had very different geographies (county through to inner London), each had a council committed to a clear vision of integration at policy level. 'Joined-up' working was already a feature of the authorities' practices, even though it might still have been a relatively new practice. In Hampshire, for example, formalised arrangements to ease communication and joint working between departments had existed for some years. In Camden, the council had long been committed to taking a corporate approach to planning and service delivery and its structure allowed for open exchange and consultation across departments.

Officers in each of these four authorities believed strongly in the value of involving the stakeholders in service planning so as to make their service more accountable, to allow communities to be more empowered and to ensure that the services provided were relevant to their users. The emphasis on working in partnership with external representatives, contained in the National Childcare Strategy, was one welcomed by these authorities. It allowed them to develop further their already established working practices.

In York, for example, which was moving from a coordinated model to an integrated one, the new authority was described as having '*a very clear vision – a focus on the customer*' whereby services were to be delivered that both assessed and met needs at customer level. This called for a breakdown of traditional departmental delineation and greater cooperation. Similarly, a senior officer in Hampshire explained that authority's philosophy: '*Hampshire has a very strong public service ethos…We want to make children's and their entire family's lives the best they can be*'. The Director of Education reinforced this policy: '*We have an integrated approach to early years issues which means that the holistic needs of the child are put first, above the sectional interests of various groups, be they political, departmental or personal*'.

While existing working practices made it easier for some authorities to develop more 'joined-up' working, they did not help others. For example, Southlea, which had adopted a collaborative model, found it difficult to implement the new national initiatives with ease. Traditional departmental demarcations were found to get in the way. In Southlea's case, these problems had been recognised and a more joined-up approach was slowly being developed.

Not all local authorities were interested in changing their existing practice to accommodate the national strategy. In Fulsham, for example, which had chosen the collaborative model, the pattern of provision in the past had a big influence on shaping the authority's present approach. For many years, private and voluntary providers had operated in isolation from each other and with limited contact with the local authority. The early years service was not a high priority in local authority policy. Some providers were even a little hostile initially towards the appointment of an Early Years Officer, fearing that the authority would use this post as a means of imposing local policy upon their provision.

National initiatives in the field of early years had sometimes had a very big impact upon an authority's choice of organisational model. Several authorities had started their journey towards more joined-up working long before the National Childcare Strategy was launched; for others, it provided the much welcomed impetus to reconsider their existing arrangements.

For Hampshire, for example, the Children Act of 1989 (GB. Statutes, 1989) had sown the seeds for developing greater inter-departmental working practices. The statutory requirements set out in the Act had provided the first opportunity for enthusiastic officers to formalise unofficial arrangements between departments and external interest groups. The

Strategy provided the additional boost to refining the structure. Hampshire found that the increased national emphasis on joined-up services and greater accessibility of centrally controlled funds provided it with a useful push towards putting its own ideas of a corporate unit for early years into practice.

For other authorities, the National Childcare Strategy was a crucial spur to action and change. In Slough, for example, local government reorganisation coupled with the launch of the Strategy provided the impetus to include the early years coordinator in their corporate management team and so encourage further integration. In Powys, the National Childcare Strategy gave the authority the chance to consider more strategic arrangements. For authorities like Southlea, the Strategy and the need to establish an EYDCP allowed officers and councillors to give greater consideration to creating a more joined-up service to meet users' needs.

Direct funding helped. Increased availability of money, direct from the DfEE, was a major help for some (like Hampshire) in restructuring the way in which they planned and delivered the early years service.

However, for authorities with traditionally separate departmental ways of working, such as Fulsham, the National Childcare Strategy did not necessarily inspire an immediate change in thinking about structure. Instead, it led them to appoint additional staff to take on the work of servicing the EYDCP and liaising with early years providers. In this case, the main providers were the voluntary and private sectors.

Local government reorganisation provided the opportunity for some authorities to explore fresh ways of organising their practice. It helped them to move either towards the greater integration of services or to decide that a coordinated model best suited the needs of their community. York, which became a unitary authority in 1996, began thinking of change at that time. Slough, which became a unitary authority in 1998, prepared for the change by employing a team of advisers and consultants to recommend an organisational strategy that would best accommodate the needs of the local population. As a result, the authority shifted from a committee structure to a cabinet model. This was thought to expand the opportunities to approach planning and policy-making from a more corporate perspective. It also facilitated greater integration of the early years service.

A local authority's geography and the need to meet very diverse needs also played some part in helping local authorities decide which organisational model was most appropriate for them. The two authorities using a coordinated approach – Powys and Wakefield – had been reorganised at quite different times. The former was expanded through reorganisation in 1996; the latter was reorganised in 1970. Both had to meet the needs of their communities, and the regeneration of both was seen to rely on greater coordination (but not integration) of their services.

Powys chose the coordinated model as the best and most flexible strategy for catering for the diverse range of families living in largely inaccessible locations and those living in densely populated areas which were nevertheless separated by a poor transport infrastructure. The coordinated model, rather than an integrated one, was seen to allow the authority to work inter-dependently with the EYDCP and to deliver appropriately diverse services to the range of end users. The authority did not wish to risk upsetting the equilibrium between the authority and local representatives by moving towards closer integration because they felt it could jeopardise the effectiveness and responsiveness of the services currently on offer. One of the reasons that Wakefield chose the coordinated model was so that the authority could better target its services in areas of greatest need.

The **political composition** of the councils in the two authorities which had adopted a collaborative model (both Conservative) seemed to be a significant factor in their choice, although by no means did politics alone dictate practice. Political attitudes were very much tied in with an authority's established working practices and their history and geography and, therefore, could not be seen in isolation from these. While the launch of the National Childcare Strategy had called for the creation of an EYDCP and personnel to service it, both these authorities ensured that they met statutory requirements, but without creating any 'joined-up' arrangements as such within the authority.

> **Local authorities had arrived at their chosen organisational models through different routes.**

The local authorities studied had started from different points in establishing their early years service. Different structures had been developed or had evolved. In some cases, a group of already committed people from different departments continued to work together; in others, responsibility was vested in one person to liaise across departments and coordinate the service. Full details are given in the case studies which appear in the next section of the report, but brief descriptions given below demonstrate the range of approaches.

In the authorities with an integrated model in place, there was usually a designated team of officers from different specialist backgrounds located in a discrete unit. These officers were also committed to the involvement of external players/providers and users. Before the establishment of their EYDCP, they had often worked together on groups such as an Under Eights Working Group, a Children and Young Persons Strategy Group, local area forums and authority-instigated consultative groups.

The authorities with the greatest extent of integration in their service were helped by the fact that a clear strategic vision of a unified service came from the very top of the authority – from councillors, Chief Executives and senior officers. The day-to-day operation of the vision was managed by dedicated and proactive officers who were also fully committed to integrated styles of working.

- In Hampshire, the fully integrated service now in practice had initially stemmed from one education officer's vision of a specialised corporate unit solely responsible for the early years service. This officer, supported by a colleague from Social Services, managed the process of change from the initial implementation stage through to the eventual day-to-day running of the unit. The council itself was fully supportive of integration and both the Directors of Education and Social Services had provided further support by allowing their staff to be deployed flexibly. Staff at all levels also shared and supported the vision.

- Camden already had a long history of taking a corporate approach to planning and service delivery. To ease the integration of early education and childcare services, senior officers used the pre-existing Under Eights Subcommittee as a basis for the development of the present committee structure. Members from three main committees formed a cross-departmental joint subcommittee for decision-making and strategy planning.

- In York, a number of officers had, for several years, shared a vision and willingness to work cross-departmentally. The launch of the National Childcare Strategy allowed the Director of Educational Services to commission a planning officer to advise on how best to establish an integrated early years service. This officer consulted and worked with a number of committed colleagues strategically to direct the process of change. Directors of the different departments were supportive and flexible and allowed officers to be deployed across departmental boundaries. A service manager and adviser were recruited to head up a discrete Early Years Unit.

- In Slough – an authority formed only in 1998 – the Chief Executive employed a restructuring team to consider a range of possible organisational structures for the authority as a whole. The chosen structure retained separate departments but had a corporate management team to ensure the integration of services. At a lower level, there were a number of policy strategy groups to facilitate integrated working arrangements. The Early Years Coordinator was part of the authority's corporate management team. Rather than managing a designated team of early years specialists, as was the case in other authorities with an integrated model, this coordinator delegated work to a range of people both within and outside the authority, including the voluntary and private sectors. The early years service was in effect a virtual entity but one which performed the task of providing integrated services across the authority from within and outside.

In authorities with a coordinated or collaborative model, a pivotal officer had been appointed to coordinate early years issues. The difference was that, in the former arrangement, that officer could usually rely on plenty of support from senior officers and cross-departmental working groups internally and from the EYDCP and other forums externally. This internal support was not so evident where the collaborative model existed.

The two authorities which had a coordinated model in place owed much of this to the National Childcare Strategy:

- Before the national emphasis on 'joined-up' working was given further impetus by the Government, departmental divisions in Powys had been fairly pronounced. The Strategy encouraged the authority to consider more strategic working arrangements. As a result, the early years service was incorporated into the departmental strategic plans and the EYDCP was placed at the centre of service planning and delivery. An Early Years Coordinator, responsible for all early years matters, was appointed to work with officers from the Education and Social Services Departments. In this case, the Partnership did not have a very high profile within the authority.

- In 1997, Wakefield authority established an Early Years and Childcare Service and appointed an education officer to coordinate it and deal with the planning and delivery of the service. The coordinator was a member of the Education Management Group.

In the two authorities where a collaborative model was in use, the process of implementation was different again:

- In Southlea, where there was some openness to the idea of change in the way services were provided, the need to investigate alternative organisational structures was recognised. Key personnel from outside the authority were appointed to head up the early years service and also to service the Partnership. Their role was to familiarise themselves with existing practice and provision in the area and then consider how best to restructure in order to facilitate or create a new early years service. This process was still ongoing at the time of the NFER research. Given that the authority tended to work very much within departmental boundaries, the work called for extensive liaison and negotiation with officers in all departments to ensure that any proposed changes to cross-departmental practice would be acceptable.

- In 1998, Fulsham authority appointed an Early Years Officer to service the EYDCP and to meet all other statutory requirements of the National Childcare Strategy. This officer was based in the Education Department. The EYDCP was the only forum in which officers from several departments seemed to work together and from which the officer could call for assistance. Any further collaboration between services was outside this officer's remit. There was no authority-wide support for an integrated or coordinated service.

> The role/position of the EYDCP in the authority's structure differed – the more integrated the organisational model, the more central was the position of the Partnership likely to be in the authority's overall structure and the greater the involvement of all key players.

In all the authorities, the EYDCP had played a crucial role in the planning and delivery of the early years service, although the degree to which different people were involved depended upon the organisational model adopted.

Positioning the EYDCP was either easy because some measure of integration already existed, or it forced people to consider new ideas about organisation and appointments. In the past, authorities now using an integrated model had usually had several active working groups or area forums concerned with early years issues. With the launch of the National Childcare Strategy, these authorities tended to place the EYDCP as a strategy group within their formal frameworks. The Partnerships were then integrated into the formal planning and decision-making structures, as in Camden and Hampshire.

While the position of EYDCP may have been less central to the authority structure where there was a coordinated model in place, the Partnerships were still proactive. For example, in Powys the Partnership had a fairly low profile within the authority and attendance by local authority officers at Partnership meetings was infrequent. Nevertheless, the Partnership was very important in the planning of the early years service. The Partnership valued its relative independence and the fact that this ensured that decisions were reached through discussion with a range of representatives from different sectors.

Despite having some support from within the authority, some early years officers in these circumstances found themselves relying heavily upon the EYDCP as a vehicle for achieving greater coordination.

The main difference between the two authorities with coordinated models was the extent to which the EYDCP was a conduit of information and support between the early years coordinator and the external providers and users. In Powys, the rural nature of the county, coupled with the dispersed population in certain areas, meant that the coordinator relied very heavily on the EYDCP to keep him informed and to disseminate information about changes in service planning and delivery. This was less true in Wakefield, an authority with a less dispersed population.

Who chaired the EYDCP was sometimes mentioned by interviewees as an important factor in the work of the Partnership. In Southlea, an authority with a collaborative model in place at the time of the research, a parent representative was the chairperson. This was seen as contributing greatly to the independence of the Partnership from the local authority and the Education Department and for ensuring that the end users' perspective was well represented. In Powys, a voluntary sector representative with a high profile locally and nationally on issues around fair play for women and quality childcare opportunities was thought to be a good person for the role of chair. This was seen to be because she could liaise easily with providers from the voluntary and private sectors and ensure that their concerns were well represented on the Partnership.

> **Different organisational models had different implications. Where the organisational structure was integrated or coordinated, the greater were the perceived benefits for officers, providers and users alike.**

The more integrated or coordinated the service was, the more streamlined and focused the provision was seen to be. Where there was a discrete Early Years Unit, a designated coordinator and structured opportunities for a dedicated team to plan strategically to meet the range of early years needs, inter-departmental tensions seemed to be absent and any duplication of provision avoided.

Collaborative arrangements created a number of difficulties for those officers with responsibility for organising early years services. Even where there was some informal cross-departmental working, it did not lead to enough coherence. Duplication of effort and work occurred where there were ineffective lines of communication and where joint strategic planning was missing.

In the authorities using either a coordinated approach or a collaborative model, the **early years coordinator's workload** was often thought to be extremely heavy. One person could rarely manage all the necessary work alone, which meant that the Partnership became the main point of contact for providers and others. This had further implications for the EYDCP.

In the mainly rural authority of Powys, members of the EYDCP were often called upon to give much support and practical help over and above their allotted time. Both the coordinator's workload and the geography of the area necessitated this style of working. While Partnership members were prepared to give their support, as they felt it ensured their (and that of other, more isolated, non-EYDCP providers) input into local authority policy development, they did acknowledge the danger that they could become overworked volunteers working as an unofficial support team for the coordinator.

In Wakefield, the size of the coordinator's workload had been recognised and the Partnership had agreed to recommend the appointment of additional local authority staff to support and extend the work of the EYDCP. It was also accepted that, in the longer term, more integration and better communication between local authority departments were necessary if the service was to be more efficient and parents were to have a single point of contact for information about a range of issues.

The Early Years Officer in Fulsham was quite overburdened by her workload. As a result of poor communication, a general absence of cross-departmental working and the fact that the early years service had a relatively low status within the authority, the officer also found herself professionally quite isolated. Her role was often misunderstood by officers, and the weight of administrative tasks she had to complete took time and attention away from other priorities.

Providers and parents were all seen to benefit greatly in the authorities using the integrated model as the organisational structure facilitated their participation. There were clear and accessible opportunities to communicate and contribute.

Through groups like the EYDCP and through commissioned development work, providers could actively help to shape policy and so ensure the relevance of the service. In turn, the authority also became much more accessible to providers, offering them a single source of advice, training and support. For example, as the Partnership chairperson in Camden (a voluntary sector representative) explained: *'We welcome the chance to participate... At long last, the Government has recognised that working with us is useful and we have a valuable part to play'*.

Parents benefited by having access to a designated team of officers who understood their concerns and could provide answers or guidance. They were given a corporate message and were not subject to a different one from each different department. In turn, the early years team was also able to monitor parents' views and needs through regular questionnaire surveys and audits. Services were, therefore, more likely to be a direct response to their needs and wishes.

Collaborative organisational strategies, by contrast, were sometimes unhelpful to both providers and parents. Providers were sometimes unsure of the precise purpose of the EYDCP or which officers could assist them with specific queries. The information provided seemed to differ between departments. There was a feeling of lack of unity. The role of the Partnership and the Early Years Officer had also raised some suspicions for providers. In Fulsham, for example, the Early Years Officer had met with some hostility from providers who supposed that her role was a means of imposing local authority policy upon their provision. It did not help that, for many years, the main providers of early years provision – the private and voluntary sectors – had not only worked in isolation from each other but also from the authority. All these factors slowed the full development of the early years service in that it was forced to work on short-term objectives in a rather *ad hoc* manner.

SUMMARY

♦ Most (62 per cent) of the local authorities which responded to Phase One of the NFER research were using a coordinated model to organise their early years service; 17 per cent had an integrated structure and 14 per cent a collaborative structure in place.

♦ There were some indications that some authorities were still developing their service – half of those with a collaborative model were moving towards a coordinated one and many with a coordinated model were considering greater integration. There was no evidence, however, to suggest that most were working towards an integrated structure or that all local authorities felt they needed to change their structures. For many, their chosen structure was that thought best suited to meet the needs of their community.

♦ Integrated structures were more common in local authorities located in small, densely populated urban areas with a high level of socio-economic deprivation (inner London and metropolitan authorities); coordinated models were more common in the counties, outer London boroughs and in the new unitary authorities. No particular types of authorities were especially associated with a collaborative approach.

♦ The elements which most often characterised local authorities that had chosen an integrated model included a commitment to and vision of integration at a corporate level; flexibility about working across departmental boundaries; a strong emphasis on involving stakeholders and the creation of a team of officers responsible for service delivery.

♦ Local authorities using the coordinated model tended to have a local council and department directors who shared a vision of coordination and who supported the structural arrangements for the early years service. There was usually a nominated officer responsible for coordination. Collaborative models were more likely to be found in authorities where there were clear lines of demarcation between local authority departments.

♦ A combination of factors had influenced an authority's choice of organisational model. These included the authority's history and geography, existing working practices, the political composition of the council, the effect of national initiatives and local government reorganisation. It was a mix of some or all of these factors which had determined choice.

♦ Local authorities had arrived at their current organisational models through different routes. In some cases, a group of already committed people from different departments had worked together for some time; in others, a restructuring team had been employed to consider a range of possible organisational structures; in yet others, responsibility was vested in one person who was responsible for organising the service and liasing between individuals and groups.

♦ Authorities with an integrated model in place tended to place the EYDCP as a strategy group within their formal frameworks; in coordinated structures, the Partnership was less central to the authority-wide structure and in collaborative structures, it tended to be quite peripheral.

♦ The more integrated the early years service was, the more visible were the benefits for local authority officers, providers and parents. The Early Years Officers in authorities which used an integrated or coordinated model tended to be less isolated than their colleagues in authorities with a collaborative structure and they felt they could often take a longer-term view of their role. Parents and providers had a clear channel for accessing and giving information.

5. CONCLUSIONS

The National Childcare Strategy published in 1998 suggested that the way forward for providing the best quality childcare was through the better integration of early education and childcare services. The Government was to provide the framework and work in partnership with local authorities, who, in turn, would work in partnership with local providers and a whole range of stakeholders. The Government did not say that integrated models of organisation were the only models that would deliver best quality services. It did, however, say that the Strategy depended on a whole host of partners working together to ensure that local needs were met. The Government has, therefore, actively urged local authorities to work in cooperation with others in the planning and delivery of children's services.

While joined-up working practices may well be best, there are several ways of joining up practice, many of which still allow a local authority to deliver its service well. Even though the NFER defined the terms 'integration', 'coordination' and 'collaboration' for the purposes of this study, it was evident that these terms could still be and were subjectively interpreted in different settings. We have seen two authorities, both of which claim to be working with an integrated model but who had quite different practices – one working very closely with external workers, the other more closely with a team of officers. Coordination, too, can mean different things, from cooperation of varying degrees of formality through to a range of corporate management initiatives.

Local authorities have taken the lead in devising new or different ways of organising their activities to allow for a more integrated approach to early years services. The latest local government reorganisation, which took place in the late 1990s, provided positive opportunities for some new unitary authorities to make a fresh start or to design more holistic services. Many of these new authorities are smaller and it could, therefore, be easier for staff from a whole range of backgrounds to work together to plan children's services.

What this piece of research has shown is that, a year or two after the launch of the National Childcare Strategy, coordinated models of organising early years services are by far the most popular. Not all local authorities aspire to have totally integrated models. Having 'significant formal arrangements in place between departments at member and officer level' (coordination) was the model that suited several types of authorities best.

While different organisational models suited different locations, integration and coordination did seem to have more benefits for all concerned than did collaborative models. The findings here certainly match those of the NCB study (McQuail and Pugh, 1995), which concluded that the key was to develop strategies for planning, resourcing and reviewing high-quality services for young children that were owned by elected members and senior officers alike. An overall vision, shared by all stakeholders, was thought to be crucial. In the two examples of the collaborative model featured in this research, this sense of ownership and shared vision seemed to be missing and the service remained somewhat fragmented.

From this study we can conclude that some of the factors that contributed most to the **successful** delivery of joined-up services included:

- a shared corporate vision and a long-term view of the role of the early years service;

- commitment and support from the top;

- the manner in which a change to integration or coordination was managed;

- a willingness to draw on expertise from outside the service and/or authority to manage the process of structural change;

- a recognition of the different 'cultures' of childcare and education, combined with a willingness to work together to achieve common goals;

- how well the model chosen for organising early years services fitted into an authority's structure and working practices;

- whether the model fitted the authority's geography and demography;

- how easy it was to deploy staff across departmental boundaries and the openness of officers to this;

- how easily the Early Years Officer could engage the help and support of colleagues;

- the relationship between the Partnership and the authority and the early years service – whether it was central or peripheral to one or both;

- the extent to which officers were prepared to work with and learn from the providers and others; and

- whether there were enough people to deliver the early education and childcare services and sufficient money to do it well.

The factors that **hampered** better coordination seemed to be:

- pronounced or entrenched resistance to cross-departmental working;

- embedded ideas about who did what;

- the placing of all responsibility for coordination on the shoulders of a single officer;

- the fact that the early years provision was given a low priority and/or a confused remit within a local authority; and

- the reluctance of certain groups to take a full part in the work of the Partnership.

If local authorities want to move further along the continuum towards greater integration, they will need to ensure that, at the very least, there is a clear understanding of what the service is trying to achieve and for whom. There will need to be a shared focus on the needs of parents; a commitment from the top; the absence of vested interests; a Partnership that is well respected, properly positioned and used; and an Early Years Coordinator who is well supported and able to meet the requirements of the job.

Integrated models certainly work very well in some instances. Although fewer than a fifth of authorities had chosen this approach, it seemed appropriate for certain kinds of authorities – especially, though not exclusively, inner London and metropolitan ones – where there is dense population and where a high concentration of early years services is provided by the local authority itself. It may be, as Owen (1995) pointed out, that the relative compactness and high levels of local authority services in such areas lend themselves more readily both to an initial vision and to the practical organisation of an integrated service.

In our examples of an integrated model, there was a strong and sustained corporate vision and a structure which enabled the smoother functioning of the service. An authority with a corporate approach to issues and which was used to working across departmental boundaries was most likely to succeed in using an integrated model. It had to be accepted, however, that in these models, more time was sometimes needed for consultation with the full range of those involved. Nevertheless, the end result was seen to justify the investment.

But integration is not necessarily the ideal way of organising services for *all* authorities and coordination may not move an authority naturally towards integration. Integration has a different agenda. After conducting several of its own studies, the NCB took the position that coordination cannot be seen as a staging post on the way to fully integrated services. It is important in itself. It can improve the quality of services sufficient to meet the needs of the local population.

The fact that over sixty per cent of local authorities in this study had adopted a coordinated approach confirms this. Coordination of services can work very well in quite different contexts and, as the case studies show, has worked very well with a dispersed community as well as with a more compact one. Coordination does allow a local authority to work very successfully with a Partnership to deliver appropriate diverse services to a wide range of users. It does not upset the equilibrium between the authority and local providers and enhances the authority's understanding of what is needed at a very local level. There must be care, however, to ensure that Partnership members are not exploited and used as unpaid civil servants. Sufficient resources from the local authority – in terms of time, people and money – will always be necessary.

What may be more important than whether an authority actually chooses an integrated or a coordinated model is the degree to which officers in different local authority departments are able to work together. Officers who come from departments with a different ethos need to be able to see the value of working together for a common goal, whether they do this through dedicated committees or through agreed arrangements between departments.

Collaborative arrangements are unlikely to deliver the perfect service. It is very difficult to avoid duplication of services if there are no formalised ways for officers in a local authority to work together across departmental boundaries. It is more difficult too for users of the service to know where to go for advice and then to be confident that the information they receive from one source will be the same as that which another source might give.

A further disadvantage of a collaborative model is that the Early Years Coordinator is more likely to be and to feel isolated and to be overworked and under pressure. Both the service and the early years unit are more likely, in a collaborative structure, to have low status and a low profile, thus creating a substantial barrier for the Coordinator. This raises the question of how far collaborative models are tenable in the longer term and whether they will be able successfully to deliver the objectives of the National Childcare Strategy.

Many early years services are still in their infancy and it is difficult to judge if they have delivered what they promised and benefited children and families as much as they hoped. Several more changes are likely to occur in the future with their associated impacts on how early years services are structured. Many services are, therefore, still developing and their effectiveness is yet to be measured. Further research would be appropriate when the structures are better embedded.

6. THE CASE STUDIES

The eight case studies in this chapter were compiled on the basis of information from two main sources:

♦ the authority's EYDCP Plan

♦ discussions with a number of the following people:

- local authority officers and elected representatives, to investigate the history of the under-fives service in their authority, the process of organisational change and current practice;

- providers' representatives, to explore their role as members of the EYDCP and their perceptions of changes and current practice;

- providers, to examine the way in which organisational changes had impacted upon their roles and services and to ascertain what their response was to current practice and to change.

Each case study is organised in a similar format and the information collected is presented under a number of subheadings:

- Introduction

- About the local authority

- Early years provision

- How the structure evolved

- How the service operates

- Impact of the service on policy and practice.

The way in which the early years and childcare service is organised in each authority is presented diagrammatically at the end of each case study.

The case studies appear in the following order:

- Examples of the integrated model: Hampshire, Camden, York and Slough

- Examples of the coordinated model: Powys, Wakefield

- Examples of the collaborative model: Southlea and Fulsham.[1]

---

[1] These two authorities preferred to appear under a pseudonym.

Hampshire Authority

Introduction

Hampshire is a county authority with a Conservative-controlled council responsible for services to a population of over 1.2 million people. It works in partnership with 11 borough/district councils. Hampshire has an integrated structure for early education and childcare services, where a team of officers work together in a discrete corporate unit. The Early Education and Childcare (EECC) Unit is headed by a long-serving education officer with direct early years and inter-agency experience and is managed jointly by the directors of Education and Social Services. Formal arrangements exist to ensure that officers from all departments contribute to the effectiveness of the service.

About the local authority

Hampshire is one of the largest county authorities in England and Wales. It remains sizeable despite local authority reorganisation in 1997, which removed Southampton and Portsmouth from the authority. Hampshire is regarded as a leafy shire county, but it does include a number of densely populated urban areas. The authority has well-established transport links, although a number of rural areas lack easy access to public transport.

The majority of families who live in the county are from White English backgrounds. While Hampshire is generally considered an affluent area, significant pockets of deprivation do exist, both in urban and rural localities. Within the rural communities, families tend to rely mainly on the agricultural sector for employment. Agricultural work is typically low paid, seasonal and concentrated in isolated communities.

Early years provision

The authority has a large number of pre-school providers. Figures for 1999–2000 show that the county provided 16,475 nursery places, through: 375 local authority nursery and reception classes and family centres; 323 private nurseries and pre- schools; 244 voluntary pre-schools and early year groups; and 47 independent schools. In addition, there were 3,472 childminders.

In broad terms, provision of early education and childcare places exceeds parental demand. Although there is a degree of geographical mismatch, wards that cannot meet the demand are compensated through extra places available in adjacent wards. The authority has a longstanding history of providing places for four-year-olds in publicly funded nursery and reception classes in schools. All four-year-olds have access to free, good-quality educational provision, within easy distance of their homes.

The main areas of concern for the Early Education and Childcare Unit were the provision for three-year-olds, out-of-school care and affordability of childcare. At the time of writing, only 5.8 per cent of the county's three-year-olds were in free nursery education. The Partnership was very keen to expand nursery places for this group, but was currently constrained by the funding allocation available.

How the structure evolved

The county council operates within a committee structure where elected representatives sit on a number of joint subcommittees.

Hampshire has long been committed to integrated working practices: family values have been a priority for a long time. Formalised arrangements have existed for many years between and within departments to facilitate coordination. The corporate Early Education and Childcare Unit (EECC Unit) was established in 1999, although it was conceptualised many years before. The increased national emphasis on coordinated services and greater accessibility of centrally controlled funds through the National Childcare Strategy provided the authority with the impetus to put its concept of a corporate unit into practice.

The authority's commitment to integration as the means of enhancing service delivery has been reflected in the council's agenda for several decades. There was consensus among interviewees about the importance that both officers and councillors placed on meeting the needs of the end user, as a senior officer explained: '*Hampshire has a strong public service ethos... We want to make children's and their entire families' lives the best they can be.*'

The Children's Services Subcommittee directly addresses issues related to early education and childcare services. Voluntary and private providers have been involved in shaping local policy for a number of years through the 20 local area forums. Representatives of the main provider groups, members of the local forums, and a range of local authority officers from various departments sit on the Early Years Development and Childcare Partnership. Elected members attend Partnership meetings as observers. The model in Hampshire makes it easier for regular meetings to take place and for two-way lines of communication to exist so as to ensure that policy-making is fully informed and streamlined.

Two prominent officers, one each from Education and Social Services, instigated the initial moves towards greater integration of early education and childcare services in the late 1980s. The Director of Education explained: '*The impetus for looking at early education and childcare in a different way came from the appointment and vision of a particular officer. From the outset, he worked very closely with Social Services... It has taken five years to see the convergence of the two departments but his will and determination were evident very early on.*'

The education officer (now the head of the EECC Unit) had a personal and professional interest in organisational theory. He saw the integration of the authority's services (for young children in particular) as the most effective method of planning and delivering services. The former adviser to Social Services (now the chairperson of the EYDCP) was supportive of her colleague's ideas. Together they began working towards integrating early years services. This process first began in 1988 when they anticipated the potential implications of the Children Act 1989 (GB. Statutes, 1989) on Education and Social Services. They predicted the overlap in the responsibilities of under-eights workers and education officers specialising in pre-school services.

Following a review of early education and childcare services by the district auditor in 1995, a report was presented to the Children's Services Subcommittee for approval. The report recommended that a corporate unit should be established to pull together the work of early education and childcare from across the two departments in order to meet increasing demands more efficiently and to make more effective use of central government funding. The recommendation was approved by the Joint Subcommittee and was subsequently endorsed by the full county council.

The Early Education and Childcare Unit became fully operational in April 1999 and is jointly managed by Education and Social Services. The Unit has sole responsibility for the coordination of early years services and has autonomous budgetary control. The head of the EECC Unit felt that his vision of an integrated organisational model had been largely realised through the Unit: '*The current Unit broadly mirrors the model in place at the DfEE, whereby early education and childcare issues are housed in the Education Department but are actually the responsibility of other departments due to the close working arrangements which amount to integration.*'

The Directors of Social Services and Education have been heavily involved in the process and are both committed to integration. This is borne out by their willingness to accommodate the needs of the Unit and the Partnership through flexible deployment of staff and by restructuring departments to allow cross-departmental working.

How the service operates

The Early Education and Childcare Unit has two major divisions, the Core Division and the Field Division (see diagram). The Core Division is based at Hampshire County Council Education Offices and is staffed by the Head of Unit, two strategic managers, four senior development officers and a number of support staff. This division is responsible for the strategic and operational planning of early education and childcare services for the entire county. It is from this base that providers and parents are able to access centrally updated information, support and advice from the Children's Information Service.

Because of the size of the authority, the day-to-day operation of the service is delivered regionally. The Field Division has 11 regional, district and borough satellite offices where teams of regulation and development officers are based. The teams are managed by one of five senior field officers who are each responsible for two or three teams. Although the senior field officers are based regionally, their direct line manager is the Strategic Manager for Regulation and Quality Assurance based in the Core Division at county headquarters. In collaboration with a number of commissioned development workers, field officers work to meet the EYDCP objectives, including the registration of pre-school providers and the provision of training and advice.

To ensure that all providers are adequately supported and involved in the service, a number of pre-school, childcare and childminding development workers from outside bodies, including the Pre-school Learning Alliance (PLA), the National Childminding Association (NCMA) and the borough/ district councils, are commissioned by the Unit. The development workers assist regional teams in supporting the full range of providers. They also have an input on policy and planning through their representation on the EYDCP and associated subgroups.

The Partnership is a very important part of the corporate EECC Unit. The number of representatives on the Partnership exceeds statutory requirements, partly because of the size of the county and partly because of the historical relationship between the authority and external parties. Through the Partnership, a range of regional concerns is identified. These are then translated into manageable objectives which the Unit must achieve. These objectives are then identified as action points and are planned as projects for completion by one of five subgroups within the Partnership. Each subgroup (which is issue-based) has a chairperson from the Partnership: these chairpersons together form the Executive. Each subgroup is supported by a senior manager from the Unit and a senior development officer. They work with the subgroup and disseminate the information. Each subgroup reports to the quarterly meeting of the Partnership.

The Director of Education felt the structural arrangements in the Unit provided an effective means of planning and delivering early education and childcare services to families in Hampshire: '*We have an integrated approach to early years issues, which means that the holistic needs of the child are put first, above the sectional interests of various groups, be they political, departmental or personal.*'

Impact of the service on policy and practice

All those interviewed in the course of our research felt that integration of early years services in Hampshire through the EECC Unit had been facilitated by commitment at all levels and by well-established joined-up working practices both in the authority and with external parties. For example, a local councillor said: '*The early years are seen as the responsibility of all departments, who work closely together to deliver a coherent system. There is visible linkage throughout the local authority from senior management to the corporate Unit and, most importantly, with local representatives.'*

The Directors of Social Services and Education had fully supported the formation of the EECC Unit. They were willing to deploy officers and ensure that they became multi-skilled in order to fulfil the demands of the wider remits of the work of the Unit. Although the majority of officers welcomed the creation of the Unit, a small number had initially been hostile. As one of the directors explained: *'There were some tensions where staff are very passionate about what they do... There were some objections to the multi-skilling and cross-departmental arrangements... They feared their particular area of interest would be lost when their work became infiltrated with broader concerns that span all departments.'* But this initial reluctance was overcome by a concerted drive to raise the profile of early years in the authority. Leading officers felt the national recognition given to early years issues also made the Unit a more attractive prospect to officers from Social Services.

The authority's officers generally welcomed the central government initiatives. They felt that the national emphasis on early years and the increased availability of funds had hastened them on their path to integration. But the officers were equally confident that the corporate Unit would have been created at some point even without the national drive. As a senior officer suggested: *'Integration has happened in Hampshire because it was always going to... but big money makes things happen more quickly.'*

Although the Unit had only been up and running for a matter of months at the time of our research, all those we interviewed felt confident that it represented the epitome of what they had been striving towards for a number of years. The Unit was felt to accommodate streamlined and holistic planning in order to provide a relevant and coherent service to providers, parents and children throughout the county of Hampshire. The councillor we interviewed summarised the advantages of the integrated Unit: *'The benefit of the* [integrated] *organisational structure is that it essentially represents a one-stop shop: parents are able to gain access to everything through one point of contact. With the Head of Unit managing policy and being supported by a committed staff with great expertise, the Unit provides the public with a coherent and accessible service.'*

Postscript

Since the NFER visit, the following developments have taken place in Hampshire: a major conference for all Hampshire providers was held; a childcare newspaper has been produced; two policy documents have been prepared – one on Play and one on Special Educational Needs/Early Years; a Children's Information Service (CIS) helpline has been established and a website is up and running.

SUMMARY

- ◆ Hampshire authority is a large shire county with a Conservative-controlled council. It has an integrated structure for the provision of early years services.

- ◆ The Head of the EECC Unit was the key driving force behind the changes. He managed the process of restructuring and was convinced that an integrated organisational model would work best.

- ◆ Local authority staff have been flexibly deployed and new structural arrangements, designed to provide a holistic early years service, have been put into place throughout the authority.

- ◆ The longstanding commitment to the integration of early years services within the authority is evidenced in the close working relationships that exist between the elected members, the local area forums, departmental directors and the head of the EECC Unit.

- ◆ The early years and childcare services provided by the 11 district and borough councils are centrally coordinated, strategically planned and monitored by the EECC Unit.

- ◆ The EECC Unit provides the focal point – a one-stop shop – for both providers and parents in terms of a unified service for information, training opportunities and support.

Hampshire Local Authority – *Structure for Early Years and Childcare Services*

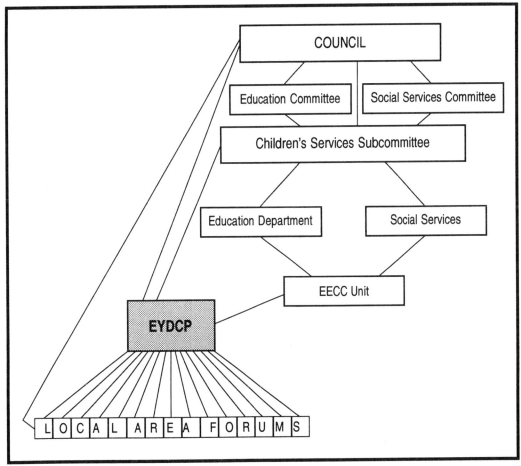

Hampshire Local Authority – *Early Education and Childcare Unit*

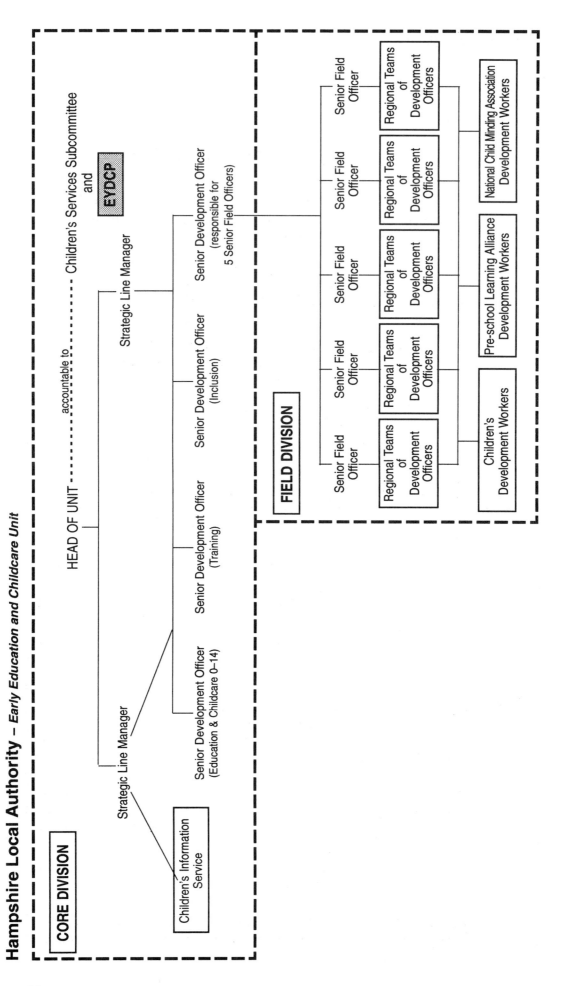

Camden Authority

Introduction

The inner London borough of Camden is a Labour-controlled authority. Early years and childcare services are planned by members and officers from several departments who work closely with health authorities and trusts, the voluntary sector and the police. The Children and Young Persons' Subcommittee of elected members is supported by a Strategy Group of officers. The EYDCP is one of a number of operational working parties that stem from the main Strategy Group.

About the local authority

Camden is one of 13 inner London boroughs and is situated to the north of the city. The area is densely populated and is very diverse in both cultural and economic terms.

The borough is characterised by a polarisation of extreme wealth and poverty. The affluent wards tend to be stable communities, while the most deprived areas have influxes of refugees, significant levels of unemployment and problems of social exclusion. Employment patterns vary from ward to ward: in some, the majority of parents have professional and managerial careers; while in the less affluent areas, the hospitality sector (i.e. restaurants, bars and hotels) provides the main source of employment. This sector is characterised by low wages and anti-social hours. Approximately half of all employees are female, a high proportion of whom are single mothers. As a consequence, there is a significant demand for childcare provision.

Because of its socio-economic deprivation and its diversity of cultures, Camden qualifies for a range of national funding grants, such as Sure Start, New Deal, Early Excellence Centres, New Opportunities Fund and the Single Regeneration Budget.

Early years provision

There are 10,980 children aged five and under in Camden. There are currently 584 registered providers of early education and childcare. The local authority provides 70 maintained nursery and reception classes, 12 pre-schools, 20 after-school clubs and 20 playschemes. The private and voluntary sectors between them provide a total of 73 pre-schools, 87 parent and toddler groups, 14 playschemes and six after-school clubs. There are also 282 registered childminders who cater for children from birth to five years. The majority of places now available for three-year-olds are in the private and voluntary sectors or in early years centres.

Despite the extensive range of provision on offer to parents in Camden, there remains a shortfall of childcare facilities to meet all parental needs.

education grant, an early years intervention team, Sure Start Camden, the Children's Information Service and the EYDCP.

The Head of Early Years (Education) is the lead officer for the Partnership. She works closely with the Head of the Play Service (Leisure and Community). They share responsibility for managing the EYDCP to ensure that Camden's policy of integration and cross-departmental working is maintained.

The EYDCP core management team is made up of a Partnership Coordinator and two development officers. The Coordinator is directly responsible for servicing the Partnership; preparing quarterly reports for the DfEE; developing strategies outlined in the Plan; and advising Partnership members about New Opportunities Fund (NOF) bidding. She also directly manages the two officers running the Children's Information Service (CIS). The CIS maintains a database of children's services in Camden, which is made available to the public and to employers in particular. The CIS also informs the Partnership about supply and demand of childcare and highlights gaps to inform future development.

The development officers are responsible for advising providers about ways to develop their provision, for exploring funding opportunities and for working with non-registered providers to develop quality standards.

Local childcare providers in Camden have had a long experience of working closely with Social Services in planning service delivery. However, historically they have had a different relationship with officers from the Education Department. Until now, education officers had not worked so collaboratively with service providers although the relationship is developing. To ensure that early years provision was dealt with holistically, personnel at all levels have had to adopt more open working practices. This was achieved to a large extent through the strategy groups.

Impact of the structure on policy and practice

Given its organisational culture and its political sympathies with central government policies, Camden has been able to implement the new national initiative with relative ease. The structures that had existed for some time in Camden were very much in line with the national emphasis on 'joined-up' working practices and so eased the implementation of the National Childcare Strategy and the inclusion of the EYDCP.

The established committee structure, which operates at all levels in the authority, lent itself well to the integration of early years and childcare services in terms of planning, consultation and delivery. An elected representative who was interviewed for this research felt that the structure enabled the authority to be flexible and responsive to new demands and to changes in personnel: '*Because the structure allows for open exchange and consultation across and within departments, effectiveness is not personality-dependent. Camden has a clear leadership and strong direction which accommodates staff turnover and the input of fresh perspectives.*'

Officers at all levels confirmed their commitment to integration. The Head of Early Years felt that cooperation and coordination, within and between departments, had positive implications for working practices: '*The integrated structure is beneficial because inter-departmental rivalries have been avoided. Through integrated strategic planning, the opportunity to consider the potential impact in terms of workload and financial implications at the outset has prevented difficulties at later stages.*' However, operating along corporate lines has presented certain challenges, especially around tight timescales. The Head of the Early Years Service explained: '*Officers are committed to integration but feel that to operate in that way requires more time than is presently allocated by government. Integration does not allow for tunnel vision. All departments have to consider the others' issues, and that takes time.*'

Voluntary sector providers appreciated the central position that the Partnership had been given in the authority's structure. The Partnership chairperson (a voluntary sector representative) felt this position signalled the important role providers played in planning policy: '*We welcome the chance to participate... At long last, the Government has recognised that working with us is useful and we have a valuable part to play.*' However, she had some reservations about the composition of the Partnership, in which over a third of members were local authority officers. There was some feeling that, despite the close working relationship the Partnership had with the local authority, on certain issues local authority policy had been imposed. She gave an example: '*Additional development workers posts had to be filled. External professionals could have filled them but we lost the battle and so they are all employed by the local authority.*'

The local authority has taken a benevolent approach to expanding and improving early education and childcare provision in Camden. By responding to the areas of most need, with the aid of central government funding, the local authority has developed provision broadly to address the needs of a range of parents in its less affluent areas. However, private providers, whose main clients were in the more affluent areas, felt their participation and involvement with the local authority had not been particularly valuable. One of the private providers interviewed felt that her relationship with the authority had not been a beneficial one: '*I joined the Partnership because I was unsure what the implications of not being involved would be. We cannot see the relevance... there is extra paperwork... They do not offer us anything we can't access elsewhere. The local authority is a support system for providers in the more deprived areas.*'

However, most of the interviewees felt that the local authority provided a high-quality early years service. Even the private provider who did not generally make use of the local authority services praised the training programme on offer: '*We are aware of the quality training programmes offered by the local authority, although we do not access them as our staff have nationally recognisable qualifications.*'

The Head of Early Years felt certain that services provided by the early years team were both relevant to and informed by the providers and parents.

43

There was consultation with providers at the EYDCP and with parents through the childcare audit and associated surveys. She felt the provider representation on the Partnership subgroups had played a key part in the planning process: '*Through the subgroups, we have identified the needs of the end user, planned and worked strategically to meet those needs and ensured best value and best fit for our customers.*'

SUMMARY

- ◆ Camden authority is an inner London borough with a Labour-controlled council.

- ◆ There is a longstanding commitment to early years services within the authority, apparent at all levels, from elected members, the chief executive and assistant chief officers to the Partnership team that delivers the service.

- ◆ The objectives of the Early Years Service concur with a broader, borough-wide regeneration strategy.

- ◆ The Early Years and Childcare Service is strategically located in the context of policy affecting children and young people.

- ◆ The established committee structure facilitates effective cross-departmental working. The structure allows officers across departments to work openly with local representatives. By involving a variety of representatives in planning and policy, services are seen to be relevant to the needs of the community.

- ◆ The integrated Early Years Service is felt to ensure greater efficiency and responsiveness to local needs. The service is able to provide information, training, support and advice on a range of childcare matters including funding. The Partnership provides a single point of contact to parents and providers.

Camden Local Authority – *Structure for Early Years and Childcare Service*

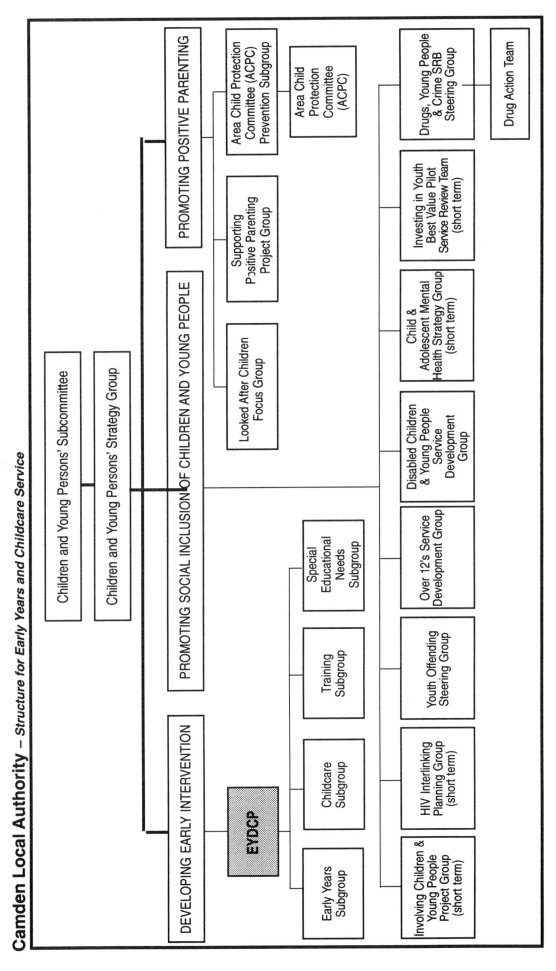

City of York Authority

Introduction

The City of York is a new unitary authority with a Labour-controlled council. The authority currently has a coordinated structure for early years education and childcare, with officers in separate departments responsible for service delivery, overseen by a working group of senior officers. The authority is about to establish an integrated service, located within Educational Services.

About the local authority

The City of York became a unitary authority in 1996. The authority covers a relatively small geographical area comprising the city and its surrounding suburbs.

The majority of families who live in the authority are from White European backgrounds. There is a low index of social deprivation in the city as a whole, although there are pockets of poverty. Traditionally, the city has had low levels of unemployment (around six per cent). Two of the largest employment sectors are food manufacturing and tourism. Despite reasonable employment levels, work in the tourist industry is seasonal and many people earn low wages. It is common for both parents to work to support their family. As a consequence, families need childcare but they often avoid using organised provision because it is relatively expensive.

Due to its low level of poverty, the authority does not qualify for funding under national initiatives targeted on deprived areas, such as Sure Start or Early Excellence Centres.

Early years provision

York currently provides 2,946 places for under-fives through 124 registered providers of early years education, including 52 maintained nursery and reception classes, 31 private nurseries, 34 playgroups, five independent schools and two special schools.

On the whole, supply of early education meets the demand from parents, although parents in some areas have difficulties accessing places.

York was not one of the authorities that benefited from government funding for three-year-olds in 1999/2000. The authority itself, therefore, provided a one-off fund of £200,000 for this provision. Government allocation for 2000/2001 is equivalent to 42 places. There are approximately 1,158 three-year-olds who require free places in the non-maintained sector.

How the structure evolved

For many years, officers shared a vision and a willingness to work cross-departmentally to achieve more efficient services. Prior to local government reorganisation, which saw the current unitary authority separated from the larger shire county of North Yorkshire, a number of senior officers were already committed to planning across departments to ensure that policy was informed from those at the grass roots. These officers established a number of informal working groups to achieve greater coordination of services.

One of these groups, the Under Eights Working Group, evolved from such an informal working party. The council then formalised the group to satisfy the requirements of the 1989 Children Act. When the group became official, membership was increased to include chief officers from the separate Educational, Social Services, Leisure and Housing Departments, together with representatives from maintained, voluntary and private childcare providers. This group then provided the authority with a strategic overview of policy and service delivery relating to provision for young children.

With the launch of the National Childcare Strategy in 1998, the Under Eights Working Group became the Early Years Development Partnership. The Under Eights Manager described the working group as '*very much the embryo for the Partnership*'. Through this group, the foundations for integration of early education and childcare services were established and links between the Partnership and the council became formalised.

A member committee known as the Children's Services Working Group was established (see diagram – former structure). A councillor representative from this committee was appointed to the Partnership. This new arrangement ensured a two-way flow of information – agendas for the Children's Services Working Group were circulated to the Partnership and when Partnership recommendations needed formal approval, they were taken to the Children's Services Working Group.

The formation of a new unitary authority in 1996 had provided the initial opportunity to reconsider existing working arrangements. The development of the National Childcare Strategy in 1998 provided further impetus for restructuring the authority's early childhood services. As The Under Eights Manager explained: '*The central government lead provided a clear strategy at national level... That has been such a strong driving force... The long history we have of working towards a unified service has suddenly become easier to achieve because of the overarching political will.*'

The Director of Educational Services, however, wanted to move toward a more integrated approach. To do this, he commissioned a planning officer, who had worked in a support role to the Partnership, to prepare a report on establishing an integrated early years and childcare service within Educational Services.

The planning officer worked with a group of officers from Educational Services, Leisure Services and Community Services to develop the structure and remit of the service in response to both local needs and national statutory requirements. There was widespread consultation and discussion. The authority also enlisted the help of the National Children's Bureau as an external source of expertise and advice. In July 1999, the Director of Educational Services submitted recommendations in a report to the Children's Services Working Group.

This report identified the need to forge a stronger identity for the early years service through a new, integrated structure for the delivery of provision. It proposed that the new service should be located in Educational Services, but with a discrete management structure and budget (see diagram – new structure). Staffing and staff responsibilities were reconceptualised. Although the plan retained many of the existing responsibilities, two new senior posts were created: an Early Years and Childcare Service Manager and a Senior Education Development Adviser (Early Years). There was also a new post for managing the Children's Information Services. The new structure had three main goals. These were to provide: an under-eights inspection and registration service; a children's information service; and early years education development. The plan was approved and recruitment began for the new posts.

How the service operates

At the time of the NFER research in 1999, the Planning Policy Officer and the Early Years Coordinator were still working closely together through the existing coordinated working arrangements (see diagram – former structure). They were jointly responsible for developing plans for the new integrated structure and for servicing the Partnership.

While the Early Years Coordinator was responsible for developing multi-agency working, the Under Eights Manager and her team of under-eights workers took responsibility for day care providers, including registration, inspection and support. The task of organising training for early years workers was taken on by an Early Years Development Consultant whose main role was Standards Fund training and support for registered providers. This consultant had also fostered links between schools and pre-school providers. For example, a primary school headteacher, interviewed in the course of this research, described how the consultant had encouraged him to set up regular meetings between schools and pre-school providers in the local area.

A Pre-school Learning Alliance Development Worker (jointly funded by the PLA, the authority and a DfEE childcare grant) had a key role in liaising with playgroups to ensure their concerns were represented to the Partnership. She made a particularly important contribution to the plans for the expansion of pre-school places in the non-maintained sector. As elsewhere, playgroups were facing closure because of competition from reception classes and nurseries. Her intervention ensured that the interests of playgroups were represented during discussions about the expansion of nursery places for three-year-olds.

The EYDCP was chaired by a lecturer in early childhood education at York University and included representatives from maintained, voluntary and private pre-school providers. Although York does not have an Early Years Forum, there was a group of parents, providers and practitioners who met under the auspices of the British Association for Early Childhood Education (BAECE). This group provided a forum for discussion for practitioners and parents and, although it had no formal role in policy-making, it provided the EYDCP with an insight into the issues affecting childcare at the grass roots.

In May 2000 (after the NFER visit), the Early Years and Childhood Service Manager and a Senior Education Development Adviser (Early Years) were due to take up their posts. It was anticipated that the Early Years and Childcare Service, as a complete and discrete part of the authority structure and in its own premises, would then have overall responsibility for implementing the EYDCP Plan and for ensuring that the views, needs and interests of all groups (providers, children, parents and the community) were reflected in policy and practice.

The Service Manager will oversee the grant allocated to the Partnership and be responsible for the delivery of the service. As well as focusing on early childhood issues, Service staff will be expected to work collaboratively with other departments to implement the authority's wider plans for children and families (such as the Health Improvement Plan).

The Service will work with the Partnership: to develop a strategy for training early years staff; to set up a childminding network; to support the development of new childcare places; to provide curriculum guidance for early years staff; and to expand out-of-school childcare. The Service will also have a strategic role in income generation by applying for regional and national grants. In the plan, it was initially envisaged that the inspection and registration of day care facilities for under-eights would be part of the new service, but the Government subsequently announced that OFSTED would take on this role. Until that time, the Under Eights team will continue to be a part of the new service.

Impact of the structure on policy and practice

The early years workers and representatives interviewed all considered that the City of York was strongly committed to providing well for young children. As the Chair of the Partnership commented: '*There is a widespread belief within York that early years are very important; they are viewed as the foundation on which all else is built.*' The aims of the local council were felt to be in tune with central government targets: this vision was shared by people at all levels in the authority, including elected members, chief officers, officers and providers.

The impetus to restructure the existing coordinated service into an integrated one had come from a clear focus on the importance of meeting the needs of service users, which would override any concerns to maintain departmental boundaries. The Under Eights Manager explained: '*The new authority had a very clear vision – a focus on the customer. We need to deliver services which assess and meet needs at the customer level. Traditional empire battles were just not going to be tolerated.*' The Planning Policy Officer also commented on the authority's pragmatic approach: '*The Education Department and the authority do try to do things as well as possible, to find solutions to problems that are good for York but are also good for the Government in terms of meeting targets.*'

The interviewees identified the formation of the original Under Eights Working Group as having been a crucial factor in establishing the positive working relationships that now underpinned the current structure. The Working Group had formed the nucleus for the Partnership and its cross-departmental approach had broken down barriers between people working in different sectors of early childhood provision. As the Under Eights Manager explained: '*There was a core group of people who had worked together in task groups – people had trained together, worked on issues and fed into Committee reports together. There is a culture of professional respect – acknowledging differences, but valuing them.*'

Placing the early years service within Educational Services was not problematic. Earlier cooperation between staff in the Community and Educational Services departments had shown how well childcare and education issues fitted together in terms of policy delivery. Staff in Community Services could see the benefit of an integrated service and were not resistant to it being placed within Educational Services. They were confident that the needs of families and childcare providers would continue to be given a high priority.

Early Years Officers did, however, accept that different traditions had informed education and childcare in the past. They were committed to ensuring that an holistic approach to young children and their families was maintained within the new structure. As the Early Years Coordinator said: '*Nationally, the educational culture is very much dominated by academic performance, whereas the culture of Community Services is more nurturing and caring. There is a need to understand that locally the Early Years Service is about things like family support and developing parenting skills (which we hope will have a result in terms of their children's ultimate achievements). Those factors must be taken into consideration too.*'

In future, the new structure should help provide a single point of contact for parents (via the Children's Information Service). Several interviewees admitted that the structure then in place was not sufficiently clear to users, as a local headteacher explained: '*I find it hard to get a clear picture of the advice and support that is available. Parents have to hit the switchboard and hope to be put through to the right person. It's a very random set-up. It will be much easier to access relevant people at the authority when they actually exist!*'

Adopting a new structure has been aided by the authority's focus on the process of change. By appointing a planning officer to oversee the introduction of a new structure, the Chief Education Officer ensured that the process itself was given a high priority, rather than being seen as an additional task for existing post holders. The planning officer drew on the expertise of other officers to devise the new structure. This process of consultation and discussion had meant that the plan was embraced by people with different perspectives and needs.

Postscript

There have been several developments since the NFER visit.

The Partnership reviewed admissions policies to infant and primary schools and consulted parents and providers on options for change. It has decided to adopt an option which means that children will start formal full-time education at the beginning of the term after their fifth birthday. This will be fully implemented by September 2003. This new policy will mean that the authority will have to have '*a careful rethink*' on how it can provide high-quality early education and childcare for three- and four-year-olds.

The Children's Information Service was launched in April 2000. The Early Years and Childcare Service was established in its new premises and the new Early Years and Childcare Manager and the Senior Education Development Adviser (Early Years) both took up their posts in May 2000.

SUMMARY

◆ The City of York is a unitary authority with a Labour-controlled council.

◆ There is a strong commitment to early years services within the authority.

◆ The authority is primarily concerned to meet the needs of service users rather than to maintain existing departmental boundaries.

◆ The present coordinated structure has facilitated close working relationships across departmental boundaries. There are officers working with different groups of service providers (schools and maintained nurseries; day care; playgroups) as well as providing a coordinated programme of training.

◆ The process of restructuring the service into an integrated one was managed by a planning officer, who consulted widely in preparing the proposals about the new service.

◆ The authority hopes that the new integrated structure will result in greater efficiency and a more flexible response to needs. There will be a single point of contact for parents (through the Children's Information Service) and for staff in educational settings (through the Early Years Adviser).

◆ Training and strategic development, including applying for Government grants, will have a stronger profile within the new service.

◆ The Early Years and Childcare Service Manager will have considerable autonomy, with responsibility for overseeing the Partnership grant. However, the Manager will be expected to work collaboratively with others to ensure effective planning and service delivery.

City of York Local Authority – *New structure for Early Years and Childcare Service*

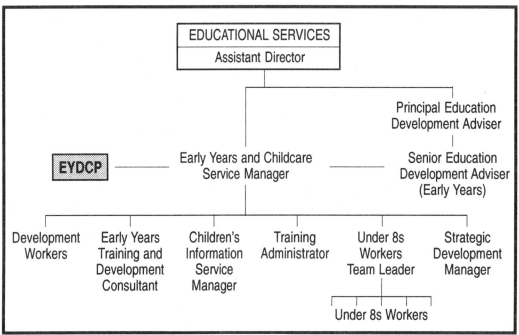

City of York Local Authority – *Former structure for Early Years and Childcare Service*

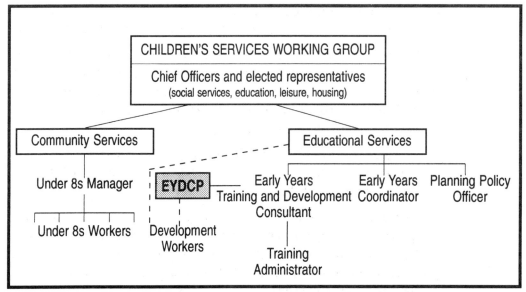

Slough Authority

Introduction

Slough Borough is a new unitary authority with a Labour-controlled council. The authority has an integrated structure for early years education and childcare. Officers from separate departments are responsible for service delivery but they are overseen by a corporate management team of senior officers. An Early Years Coordinator is part of the corporate management team and liaises with officers from all departments to integrate early years matters with other policy areas. Local authority early years policy is conveyed to and negotiated with members of the Partnership through the Coordinator. Similarly, the views of the EYDCP are channelled to the local authority through the Coordinator.

About the local authority

Slough Borough Council gained unitary status in 1998. Before that, it was part of Berkshire County Council.

Slough is a geographically large and densely populated urban borough, 21 miles west of London. The borough has a surrounding green belt, which separates it from neighbouring local authorities. Families living in the authority are drawn from a number of racial and cultural groups. Approximately a third of families who live in Slough have ethnic minority origins, mainly Indian, Pakistani and Black African/Caribbean. There are also growing numbers of children from refugee backgrounds living in certain areas of Slough.

Traditionally, the main source of employment in Slough has been the manufacturing industry. However, the last two decades have seen a 54 per cent decline in the local manufacturing sector, which has contributed to unemployment in the borough. While the fall in manufacturing jobs has, in part, been offset by the growth in service and retail sectors, there is a mismatch of skills. Many companies have been recruiting from outside the borough. The unemployment rate is currently around three per cent and a third of this is long-term. Although there is a relatively small proportion of lone parent families, the majority of these are headed by economically inactive mothers. This contributes to the need for subsidised childcare.

Accessibility of childcare is not a problem for the majority of parents – transport services are available and Slough is committed to ensuring that early years provision is available to families within a two-mile radius of their home.

Given its multiracial character and its socio-economic diversity, Slough is eligible for funding under national initiatives to tackle social exclusion, such as Sure Start and Early Excellence Centres.

Early years provision

There are approximately 8,000 under-fives in the borough. The authority currently provides places for all of its four-year-olds and for 50 per cent of its three-year-olds, through 17 LEA nursery classes, five LEA nursery schools, 18 reception classes, eight local authority day nurseries, 11 playgroups, one private nursery, two independent schools and 200 registered childminders. The DfEE has provided funding for an extra 244 places for three-year-olds from 2000.

How the structure evolved

Before Slough became a unitary authority in 1998, local councillors spent a number of months planning the organisational structure that now operates in the authority. Under the direction of the Chief Executive, the council employed a group of advisers, consultants and a restructuring team to establish an organisational strategy that would best accommodate the needs of the local population. The resulting structure included a corporate management team of senior officers to ensure that coordination of services took place at all levels from the top down.

At the time of our research in 1999, the local council was in the process of shifting from a committee structure to a cabinet model. Under the committee structure, the Social Services and Education Committees met on a regular basis to discuss issues of mutual interest and to reach decisions on planning and policy from a joint perspective. The new cabinet, which replaces the committees, is made up of an executive group of six local councillors. A number of our interviewees felt that this new cabinet model would provide the opportunity for local councillors, in conjunction with senior officers, to approach planning and policy from a more corporate perspective.

The council has devised a discrete number of key policy priorities. These include equality of opportunity; community development; economic development; healthy environment and social justice. The aim of these priorities is to provide continuity of planning and policy across and within departments. As such, every major proposal and local initiative, including the Partnership, has to relate to the policy principles set out by the council.

The early years policy adheres to the broad priorities set out by the council but also relates to national and international legislation, including the 1989 Children Act, the NHS and Community Care Act 1990 and the United Nations Convention on the Rights of the Child.

The corporate management team of senior officers manages all local authority services, but separate departments continue to exist at the operational level. These include Social Services, Community Services, Education and Housing. Although staff are located in different places and have different titles, integration occurs at officer level and is facilitated through a number of shared projects. One such example is the Quality and Lifelong Learning Strategy. This project incorporates the council's key policy principles, is directed by the corporate management team and involves officers from all departments in its delivery. The range of ongoing strategies and projects necessitates integrated working practices and strategic planning at all levels.

In response to the National Childcare Strategy, the Chief Executive, senior officers and local councillors felt that an Early Years Coordinator should be employed to service the Early Years Development and Childcare Partnership and to be part of the corporate management team. They believed that this post would ensure integration of service planning and delivery between the officers and the Partnership. The Coordinator therefore plays a central role in integrating the work of all departments on early years matters.

Before the Partnership was established, there was a longstanding relationship between the local authority and local early years representatives through the Under Eights Group. This then became the Early Years Forum. The Forum includes 40 representatives from voluntary, private and statutory organisations concerned with the expansion and quality of early years services. It continues to maintain links with the authority through membership of the Partnership and through close liaison with the Early Years Coordinator.

How the service operates

The Early Years Service is integral to a number of the local authority strategies but is most prominent in the Quality and Lifelong Learning (QLLL) Strand. Policy imperatives such as early intervention, family education and improving female employment opportunities clearly fall within the remit of the Service. The Early Years Coordinator is one of the key local authority players in the QLLL strategy. Her role is to help ensure that early intervention takes place where necessary so as to prevent social difficulties that children may face in later life. As an Assistant Chief Education Officer explained: '*The Early Years Coordinator is seen as central and her title really does convey exactly what she does. She coordinates the work of the different departments and the interests of a range of end users.*'

From wide consultation with Partnership members and through the local childcare audit, targets were identified for the improvement and expansion of early education and childcare services in Slough.

The Early Years Coordinator is assigned primary responsibility for servicing the Partnership, which itself comprises the full range of requisite members. Of the 33 members, approximately a third are from the local authority. In addition to officers specialising in early years education, there are officers from: Social Services, the Health Authority, Pupil Services, Children's and Families' Services, Play Services, Educational Psychology Services, Teaching and Support Services and Equality Services. These officers, along with representatives from voluntary, private and public providers, are also represented on the Partnership subgroups. Each subgroup convenes to identify targets for one of a range of issues, such as: training; networking services; providing information; and enhancing existing provision for young children with special needs. The work of the subgroups is fed back to the full Partnership, reviewed by the Coordinator and then presented to the Early Years Management Group for approval before it reaches the Council.

Once the Partnership subgroups have identified strategic solutions to a particular area, the Early Years Coordinator delegates the necessary work to appropriate personnel, either from organisations represented on the Partnership or to officers. For example, registration of pre-school settings and any work on the database of childminders in the borough would go to the Under Eights Team in Social Services, while work on developing a community childminding network would go to the National Childminding Association (NCMA) manager because the Partnership has a service-level agreement with the Association.

The Partnership also has a service-level agreement with the Pre-school Learning Alliance. Through the Childcare Grant and via local authority funding, a senior development worker and an area development worker have been commissioned to work with pre-schools, provide a liaison point and deliver a training programme to the full range of early education and childcare providers in the borough. The authority itself also provides a comprehensive training programme for all providers, which is delivered by local colleges, an LEA Professional Development Centre and two training centres based at local nurseries. This programme is widely disseminated throughout the authority via the Partnership.

The need for greater provision 'wrap-around' to the existing pre-school opening hours was identified through the Partnership and the childcare audit. The Out-of-School Initiative is managed by the Coordinator and informed by the Partnership, but another commissioned development worker (from the Children's Information Centre, based in Reading) is responsible for its day-to-day operation.

The commissioned development workers are based in their respective organisational offices but address the local needs of Slough through the Partnership and in conjunction with the Coordinator. Each development worker reports directly to the Coordinator but is ultimately answerable to the Partnership.

In addition to the Education, Social Services and Community Services Departments, other authority departments also assist in delivering early education and childcare services. There are two Early Years Centres in Slough based in two of the more deprived areas of the borough. Representatives from a range of voluntary and private organisations are available at the Centres to provide families with advice, support and training. Officers from each authority department are part of the management group of the Centres. The health authority is also an integral part of the Partnership's dissemination strategy. Through their health visitors, families receive up-to-date information about provision in the area – both early education and childcare services and more general family-focused provision.

Despite the number of development workers available to assist the Early Years Coordinator, she retains a sizeable workload. This was recognised by her line manager, an Assistant Chief Education Officer (ACEO): '*We are aware that the Early Years Coordinator's workload is a heavy one, so on occasion we appoint people to assist her... For example, a headteacher was seconded to conduct the audit of childcare provision as required by the Plan.*'

The Early Years Service, then, is somewhat of a '*virtual service*'. The Coordinator has the professional autonomy to 'broker' work to relevant personnel and she is supported by a management team comprising Assistant Chief Officers from across departments.

Impact of the structure on policy and practice

All of the interviewees agreed that the integrated structure in place in Slough had stemmed primarily from the vision and forward planning of the Chief Executive and the central role played by the Early Years Coordinator in translating that vision into practice. Some other significant factors were also identified as having helped to structure the integrated working arrangements in Slough – local authority reorganisation, wide consultation, the importance attributed to early childcare and the early appointment of a Coordinator.

Gaining unitary status in 1998 had provided the authority with the opportunity to explore a range of different organisational strategies. This process was well informed by the restructuring experts employed by the Chief Executive. The restructuring team set about identifying local needs through extensive consultation. As the Early Years Coordinator explained: '*As well as providing very strong leadership, she* [the Chief Executive] *allocated resources for a restructuring team... They were very good consultants who did a lot of the spade work prior to us becoming a unitary authority... There was a lot of consultation, a lot of information gathering.*'

Now that the local authority structure is established, the directors of each department are located in a corporate suite. They manage the entire authority using a team approach, promoting arrangements for cross-departmental work, integrated planning and delivery. The advantages of such arrangements were outlined by an elected member: '*Provision of services will benefit from integration because departments are not competing for the same money or duplicating what has been done by another department.*'

The restructuring team, the Chief Executive and the directors of each department regard early years provision as important, partly because of the national emphasis on childcare and partly because it forms the basis of a number of authority-wide strategies such as Quality Life Long Learning Strategy and the Social Inclusion Portfolio. The recognition of the key role played by the Early Years Service was evident in the early appointment of the Coordinator to integrate the services. As the Early Years Coordinator explained: '*My post was the very first to be advertised when we became a unitary; I was the first officer to be appointed, even before the Chief Officers. Early Years was seen as an important area to develop. The Coordinator needed to be in post to get everything set up and ready.*'

However, there were some tensions surrounding the line management of the Coordinator. Although the Coordinator is officially part of the corporate management team, the post is funded by the Education Department and her direct line manager should be an ACEO. To offset this tension, and in recognition of the corporate role that the Early Years Service performs, the Coordinator reports to an Early Years Management Group of ACEOs from Social Services, Community Services and the Education Departments. The Coordinator expressed her concerns about possible misconceptions: '*Some people refer to me as an Education Officer and I'm not. I am a local government officer with a corporate role and I continually have to spell that out. I suppose if I was based in the corporate suite, the message would be clearer… It would be easier for people to recognise that I am the Early Years Coordinator. However, the Education Department is the most appropriate base for my work.*'

The process of change in Slough has been facilitated by clear leadership, specifically appointed personnel and the identification of the needs of local communities. The authority continues to adapt working practices in the light of local need. The ongoing process of consultation and involvement of local organisations has ensured that provision is well informed and appropriately delivered by providers in conjunction with the local authority.

Postscript

Since the NFER visit, Slough has developed a training strategy to try to meet recruitment difficulties. The authority is also planning to work with local employers on family-friendly policies.

SUMMARY

♦ Slough borough is a new unitary authority with a Labour-controlled council.

♦ Gaining new unitary status provided the authority with an opportunity to identify the most appropriate organisational strategy to meet the needs of service users.

♦ The authority set about a period of consultation before establishing a corporate organisational structure.

♦ Slough has a number of key policy priorities with which all initiatives have to concur. The Early Years Service does that and is well supported.

♦ The authority has integrated arrangements in place for the delivery of early education and childcare services.

♦ A designated officer was appointed to service the EYDCP and to coordinate early years matters among all local authority departments and relevant external organisations. The Coordinator is part of the corporate management team.

◆ The Early Years Service is a 'virtual' service managed by the Early Years Coordinator. She delegates work to a number of personnel both within the local authority and to development workers from voluntary and private organisations.

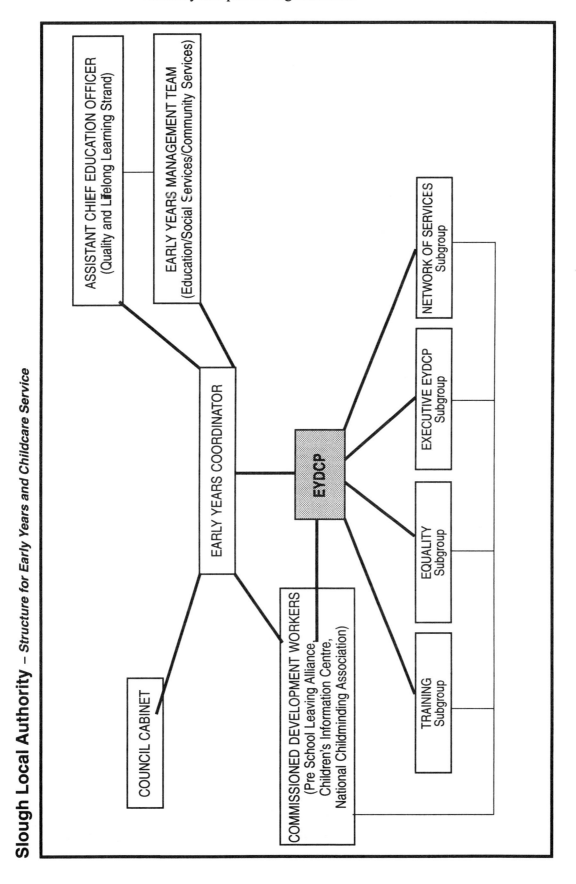

Slough Local Authority – *Structure for Early Years and Childcare Service*

Powys Authority

Introduction

Powys, like the other 21 councils in Wales, is a unitary authority. It is led by independent councillors. The authority has a coordinated structure for early years education and childcare, with officers from separate departments responsible for the service. An Early Years Coordinator and the EYDCP deliver the service. It is overseen by a senior management team and a working group of senior officers, local councillors and local early years representatives.

About the local authority

Powys encompasses a large geographic area covering most of mid Wales. It comprises five sparsely populated towns and a number of dispersed agricultural communities. Following local government reorganisation in 1996, the county of Powys became a unitary authority, with a single council and three shire committees which take some responsibility for the local planning of services.

Families in Powys are overwhelmingly from White European backgrounds and the majority speak both English and Welsh. Officially, the county has a low index of social deprivation, but the true situation is masked by measurement factors such as car ownership – a necessity for many in this rural part of the country. Although unemployment levels are generally low, there is a problem of long-term unemployment. The major source of employment is the agricultural sector, where wages are low and work is often seasonal. Given the sparsity of population and the lack of easy access to larger towns for many rural families, childcare is often inconvenient to reach and relatively expensive. It is therefore common for families to arrange informal childcare with extended family and friends and to access sessional care when it is available or convenient.

Early years provision

There are approximately 7,000 under-fives in Powys. The authority currently provides places for 98 per cent of its four-year-olds in its 105 infant schools, each of which has a nursery and/or a reception class attached. There are 1,500 places in pre-school playgroups, approximately 400 places within private day nurseries (some Welsh, but most English-speaking) and over 500 places provided by some 150 registered childminders. At the time of writing, the LEA and the EYDCP were awaiting the result of consultations by the National Assembly for Wales on future provision for three-year-olds.

Supply of childcare places broadly meets parental demand. There is a tradition of parents selecting a range of provision for their children according to affordability, availability and accessibility. The difficulty of accessing provision is a significant factor affecting the take-up of places: families send their children to school at the earliest opportunity because organised transport is available.

How the structure evolved

Before the current national emphasis on 'joined-up working', departmental divisions in Powys had been very pronounced with the result that responsibilities and planning were clearly delineated. A number of interviewees felt that, previously, the authority had lacked a broad, clear and shared purpose and vision.

Unlike other councils in the study, Powys Council is made up of independent councillors who represent the parochial interests of their own constituents. Elected representatives chair departmental committees and so deal with any cross-departmental and cross-committee issues. The chairs of the Education, Social Services, Housing, Leisure and Community and Environmental Health Committees meet to coordinate plans from a corporate angle. The elected representative interviewed felt the committee structure provided an authority-wide vision grounded in 'the needs of the customer' and 'embedded in a number of authority-wide strategies', the majority of which encompass early years issues.

Historically, there had been a number and range of discussion forums in the local authority designed to achieve greater coordination. The Early Years Forum was one such group, made up of committee chairs, local authority officers, an early years adviser and representatives of external agencies. Inter-departmental working that had taken place at senior management level through the Forum now happens via the Partnership.

There is a strong belief among senior officers in the value of working in partnership with other organisations – both local and national – based in Powys. There is a commitment to working collectively both with those who deliver and those who receive services to ensure that provision is focused, relevant and useful. The local authority officers interviewed felt it was important to allow practitioners to have ownership over the planning and delivery of services, while their role was to provide support and guidance.

Departmental strategic plans provide a clear set of objectives to be met in substantive areas. One such plan is for early years education. The plan sets out the timing, resources, monitoring, evaluation and staffing for each objective. The launch of the National Childcare Strategy in 1998 provided the authority with the opportunity to consider more strategic working arrangements. A decision was taken to place the Early Years Development and Childcare Partnership at the centre of service planning and delivery.

The Early Years Service has overall responsibility for implementing the Early Years Development and Childcare Plan and for ensuring that local views and needs are reflected in planning and provision. The Service encompasses the Partnership and together they have developed a training strategy for early years providers. The Service is also responsible for income generation via bidding for Welsh and other grants.

The Early Years Education objectives (from the strategic plan) are now primarily the responsibility of the Early Years Coordinator. He works with the Early Years Adviser (for Schools) and an Assistant Director. Officers from other areas and departments are required to contribute where necessary. In addition to meeting the objectives of the strategic plan, the Early Years Coordinator is also responsible for servicing the Partnership.

As a relative newcomer to the authority, the Coordinator works closely with the Early Years Adviser to forge links with key personnel on the council and with officers in the authority. The Coordinator is supported by a Management Support Group made up of local authority officers, the chair and vice chair of the Partnership.

Decisions reached by the Partnership are reported back to the Education and Social Services Committees and/or to the full council. Ultimately, the work of the Partnership is presented to the Welsh Assembly for approval.

How the service operates

The Welsh Assembly has set a national agenda in which the customers' needs are paramount. In keeping with this, the child is the focus of the Early Years Service in Powys. The needs of the customer are identified via the Partnership and the childcare audit. These are used to inform the planning, policy and delivery of service. This approach is believed to ensure 'best fit' for children and best value for the authority.

Officers regard children's services as the crucial starting point for extending equality of opportunity to the population of Powys. Supporting children from an early age is perceived to have benefits for the community as a whole. Early years issues, therefore, feature as part of larger authority-wide strategies, such as the Anti-Poverty Strategy.

At the time of the NFER visit in 1999, the early childhood education and care service was being delivered predominantly by officers in the Education Department, although staff from Social Services participated on occasion in a monitoring capacity. The objectives set out in the Education Strategic Plan (equivalent to the Education Development Plan in English authorities) apportioned primary responsibility for the service to the Early Years Coordinator and the Partnership.

Despite the national imperative to expand early education and childcare places, the Partnership decided to place the emphasis on improving the quality of existing provision rather than expanding it. This was to be achieved by the four main objectives in the Education Strategic Plan, which were to: raise standards of provision; improve the quality of education provided; improve management and efficiency; and improve arrangements for pupils' spiritual, moral, social and cultural development.

The Management Support Group, established to assist the Coordinator in servicing the Partnership, has taken a very hands-off approach to running the service. The practicalities are left to the Coordinator and the more proactive members of the EYDCP, especially the chairperson. Working groups on the Partnership develop strategies for improvement which are fed to the local authority through the Coordinator.

A local voluntary sector representative chairs the EYDCP. She has a high profile both locally and nationally through her organisation *Chwarae Teg (Fair Play)*, which aims to improve female employment and the quality of childcare opportunities in Wales. As chairperson, she has a key role in liaising with the voluntary and private providers while ensuring that the concerns of all providers are effectively represented on the Partnership.

The Partnership enjoys considerable autonomy because it sits on the periphery of the local authority structure yet is central to the delivery of early years provision (see diagram). Its independence ensures that decisions are reached through the collaboration of a range of representatives from different sectors across the authority. This shared decision-making with local providers and others is thought to ensure that the best solutions are reached for end users in Powys. Local knowledge is important where the population is spread out and the infrastructure is not always adequate.

Despite its important role in terms of planning and delivering early years services, the Partnership has a low profile within the local authority. Attendance at Partnership meetings by a number of local authority officers is infrequent. This reduces its status and affects its power to bring about changes. In an attempt to address the situation, the Partnership has made a series of presentations to local authority committees. It has also adopted a marketing strategy and developed a number of road shows to help raise awareness among officers, providers and parents.

Long-term planning and development are hampered by the uncertainty of funding. The Partnership has to convince the Welsh Assembly of the need to review the authority's funding allocation. Until this happens, the Partnership is forced to focus mainly on short-term solutions to the immediate issues it faces.

Impact of the structure on policy and practice

The early years representatives, local authority officers and local councillors involved in the NFER research felt that, while the EYDCP had been the key driving force behind the coordination of service delivery, there were also other significant factors which had contributed to the success of the Early Years Service.

The corporate vision of the council, provided through its committee structure, clearly set out a number of strategies which identified shared priorities that needed to be tackled by the authority and significant other local representatives. Although elected representatives had not been proactive as members of the Partnership, they were fully supportive of the approach that had been adopted.

Senior officers had also been supportive of the role that Partnership members had played in planning and delivery. The commitment to ensuring that local authority policy would be informed from the bottom up was borne out by their decision to put the EYDCP at the centre of the Early Years Service. The Chairperson explained: '*The local authority has made public its commitment to allow key interest parties, who are in tune with grass roots operation, to work closely and openly with local government.*'

Even though there was overwhelming satisfaction that local representatives very were active in service planning, there was some concern about the workload for Partnership members, as the Chairperson recognised: '*The effective working of the early years service is dependent upon goodwill and voluntary commitment of Partnership members. There is a danger they may have effectively become unpaid civil servants.*'

Many of the participants in the research felt that the Government's Childcare Strategy had provided the impetus for positive changes in working relationships. The Strategy had allowed local providers to become more empowered to inform and shape policy and thereby influence service delivery. However, some tensions were acknowledged between Government policy and the needs of an authority like Powys. The Coordinator was critical of the perceived tailoring of policy to meet the needs of urban authorities rather than those with a rural, dispersed population: '*Central government directives focus on issues faced by urban authorities. Both central government and the Welsh Assembly fail to recognise the unique difficulties the Powys Partnership faces.*'

There was optimism about placing the Partnership at the heart of the Early Years Service. It enabled provision to be more relevant. The Early Years Adviser felt that the service would also eventually impact on the wider work of the authority by helping to meet broader targets aimed at enhancing the life chances of people living in the authority. She explained: '*The Partnership's success in coordinating and raising the quality of* [early years] *provision has implications for officers...* [It will] *reduce their workload on long-term problems that may stem from an inadequate start in life such as poor educational attainment, unemployment or criminal behaviour.*'

The increased coordination of services, achieved through the work of the Coordinator and the EYDCP, had ensured that the targets in the departmental Strategic Plan were being met. Providers confirmed that they were receiving information on training and other key issues via their Partnership representatives and that they had become more aware of opportunities available to them and their staff. As the Early Years Adviser noted: '*The Partnership has been able to support workers from all sectors in a more focused way.*'

Parents had also received more focused attention through the work of the Early Years Service. Partnership members felt they were managing to plan and cater effectively for the diverse range of parental needs in their very diverse authority.

Postscript

The main development since the NFER visit has been the production of an EYDCP Plan for 2000–2003.

SUMMARY

♦ Powys is a unitary authority in Wales, led by independent councillors.

♦ There is commitment to early years and childcare at many levels in the authority, apparent in the corporate vision provided by the local council; in the Education Strategic Plan; and in the appointment of an Early Years Coordinator.

♦ The authority is concerned with meeting the needs of the 'customer' through its committee structure and via the Partnership. However, some departmental boundaries continue to exist.

♦ Powys opted for a coordinated approach to the provision of early education and childcare as this was thought the most appropriate arrangement for a geographically large authority with a dispersed population. The authority officers considered it important that practitioners had ownership over the planning and delivery of services, while they provided support and guidance.

♦ Primary responsibility for delivering the Early Years Service rests with the Coordinator and the Partnership.

♦ Partnership members work closely with the Coordinator and are an invaluable source of information. The Partnership has facilitated close working relationships between providers and the Early Years Service.

♦ Even though the Partnership has a great deal of autonomy which was felt to be important in terms of planning service delivery in a rural authority, it has a low profile within the authority. This, plus uncertainty about future funding, has hampered longer-term development plans.

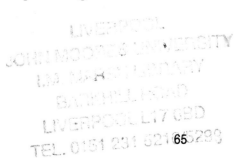

Powys Local Authority – *Structure for Early Years and Childcare Service*

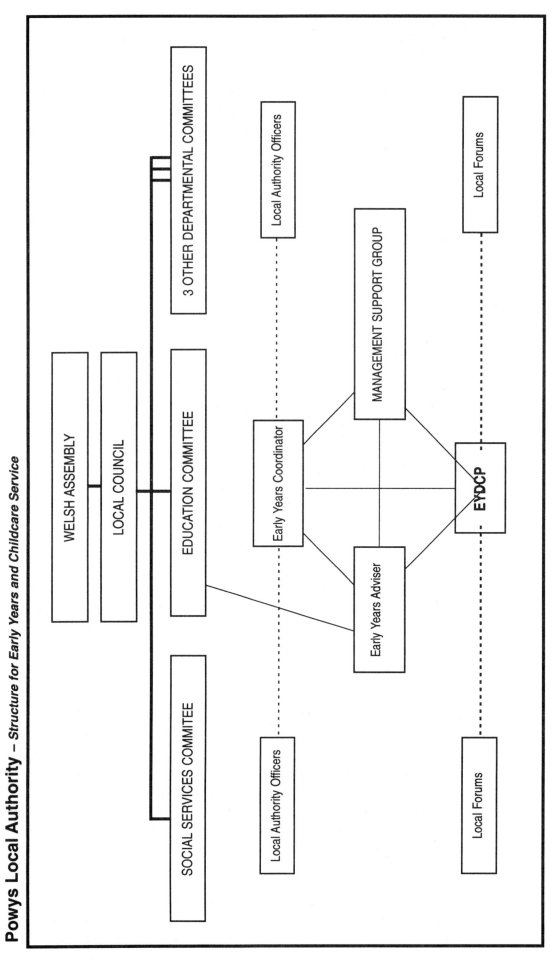

The Metropolitan Borough of Wakefield

Introduction

Wakefield is a metropolitan authority with a Labour-controlled council. The authority has been developing a coordinated structure for early years education and childcare, with both Education and Social Services involved in service delivery. There is an Education Officer with specific responsibility for coordinating early years and childcare, based in the Education Department. The authority also has a childcare information service which is run by an independent organisation.

About the local authority

Wakefield is one of five local district authorities in the West Yorkshire metropolitan area. These districts were established nearly three decades ago during a major reorganisation of local government. Wakefield is composed almost equally of rural and urban areas and has a well-established system of public transport, although there are problems of urban congestion and some rural areas lack access to public transport.

The majority of families living in the authority are from White European backgrounds. Although not among the most economically deprived in England, the area has suffered from an economic downturn due to the decline of mining and heavy industry. Many people are employed in the public services. Private employers tend to be small businesses employing fewer than 12 people, although several companies have recently established large warehouse distribution centres in the area. As a result of the decline of heavy industry, there has been a shift from full-time employment to temporary and part-time positions, most of which are taken by women. Certain areas of the borough suffer from severe problems of unemployment and poverty.

Early years provision

There are approximately 24,450 children aged five and under in the district. In Wakefield, places are provided for 100 per cent of four-year-olds and 78 per cent of three-year-olds. The local authority has 37 pre-five classes, 72 nursery classes, four nursery schools, and one pre-five centre. The voluntary and private sectors provide 1,126 funded early education places through 18 playgroups and 30 private nurseries. There are also 340 registered childminders in the borough.

How the structure evolved

Until recently, the council had a traditional committee structure, with separate committees responsible for Education, Social Services, Housing and Environmental Services. Although there are still four departments at officer level, the borough adopted a 'cabinet' style of policy-making in

1999. There is a cabinet committee, made up of elected members, that meets once a week and the full council that meets once a month. This means that while departmental boundaries are still in evidence, they are less strongly marked than before.

To coincide with the establishment of the Early Years Development and Childcare Partnership, the borough set up a Young Children's Coordinating Group (YCCG) to ensure coordinated support for early years across all council departments. This group is made up of all the officers with an interest in young children and their families. It evolved from a longstanding Children's Services Working Group, which had a narrower brief, but included councillors as well as officers. When the Partnership was formed, it was decided that the councillors should represent the local authority on the Partnership, with officers taking a supporting role. At present, the role of the Young Children's Coordinating Group is being reviewed. As the work of the EYDCP becomes more established, it is hoped that the YCCG will be able to concentrate more clearly on internal issues.

The YCCG meets every six weeks or so to discuss issues affecting young children. At the time of our visit, the Group was chaired by a representative from Social Services.

How the service operates

In 1997, the authority established an Early Years and Childcare Service within the Education Service and appointed an Education Officer for Early Years and Childcare. Prior to that, the early years service came within the remit of an education officer who had a number of other areas of responsibility. The Early Years and Childcare Service is located in the Pupil and Parent Services branch of the Education Department. The post of Education Officer for Early Years and Childcare was filled by a former nursery teacher/early years advisory teacher.

Over the past year, the Early Years and Childcare Service has developed a team of people who work to support both the EYDCP and other local authority initiatives. The team is being relocated so that all staff are in the same place. This will enable the service to operate in a more coordinated way. A Primary Adviser, with special responsibility for early years, works with the team to coordinate training for early years education. Standards Fund money is used to employ an Early Years Consultant and a team of leading teachers.

The Education Officer for Early Years and Childcare is a member of the Education Management Group. This group is made up of officers drawn from the three branches of the Education Department, who meet together once a month to exchange information and discuss issues of common interest.

Since her appointment, the Education Officer for Early Years and Childcare has taken the lead responsibility for supporting the work of the EYDCP, which has involved writing and implementing the Partnership's plan.

However, this has placed considerable demands on her time. In recognition of this, the Partnership is soon to appoint a manager who will work within the Early Years and Childcare Service. The new appointment will enable the Education Officer for Early Years and Childcare to devote more time to other areas of her brief. In the past year, her local authority work has included: a review of the local authority admissions policy for early years; a review of the authority's nursery schools; the submission of a bid for an Early Excellence Centre; and membership of the Sure Start steering group.

The Education Officer for Early Years and Childcare has also been involved in preparing specific guidance for parents on the range of provision for early years education and childcare. She hopes to build links with colleagues in the health authority in order to ensure distribution of written guidance to all parents as soon as possible after the birth of their child.

The Education Officer for Early Years and Childcare and the Assistant Chief Education Officer are the main points of contact between the Partnership and the authority. Social Services are also represented at Partnership meetings, principally through the Head of Children's Services.

The EYDCP Chairperson is someone with wide-ranging interests in education and the early years. She represents the Catholic Schools on the Partnership, but is also a local councillor who previously held the post of deputy chair of education. She is a director on the board of an independent organisation that provides the authority's Children's Information Service. When asked for her views on the local authority's strategy for young children, the Partnership Chair explained that she considered the interests of young children to be part of a broader policy agenda for people living in the borough: '*We see the early years as part of a lifelong learning strategy. Our overriding aim is to benefit entire families from all backgrounds and to improve the quality of life for citizens in Wakefield.*'

The Partnership has an approximately equal balance between public, private and voluntary sector representatives. A strong feature of the Partnership is the prominent role played by representatives from the private and voluntary sectors, some of whom chair subgroups. This commitment to and from the private and voluntary sectors has been further demonstrated through the employment of a team of childcare development workers from a range of sectors to develop new places and to support early childhood providers. (In future, the coordination of their work will be the responsibility of the new Partnership manager.)

The Partnership's main purpose is to implement the central government agenda of developing new childcare places and integrating care and education. However, the task of integrating care and education is not made easy by the maintenance of separate funding sources for education and childcare. The Partnership has received funding for free early education places for three-year-olds, which was used to provide new places in the maintained, private and voluntary sectors. This was achieved by setting up a subgroup of members from all sectors and was felt to be a good example of Partnership working.

As the Partnership has become established, it is now beginning to take a lead role in representing the interests of young children in the council's bids for central government funds. For example, when the council was invited to bid for a pilot project under the Early Excellence Centres initiative, the Education Officer for Early Years and Childcare worked closely with representatives from the Partnership to put together their proposal to establish a network of Early Excellence Centres in the authority.

Impact of the structure on policy and practice

The council has made a series of commitments to early childhood education in its corporate goals. The Partnership is a major focus for their coordination. However, as in other authorities, the fact that the Partnership is a voluntary body imposes limitations on the number of different tasks it can be expected to complete.

All parties hope that the coordinated structure for early education and childcare in Wakefield will lead to less duplication and better targeting of services on areas in greatest need. In the longer term, joint planning between education and childcare services should mean that the two services can be delivered on the same site (e.g. in an Early Excellence Centre) so that parents do not have to transport their children between pre-school and childcare. The Assistant Chief Education Officer explained that parents would soon begin to reap the benefits of this coordinated approach: '*The relationship between education and childcare providing joined-up services will begin to impact on parents fairly shortly. They won't recognise that we are joined up ... All they will be able to see is that they can have education and childcare on the same premises.*'

However, it will take some time to form the working relationships within the authority to underpin the strategic goal of offering a fully integrated service. As the Education Officer for Early Years and Childcare said: '*We need more staff and time to give to this area of work so we could bring it closer to the top of the agenda. We need to set up systems whereby people share information and network more effectively than we have done in the past.*' It is important to this officer that she has involved officers from other departments in joint planning. Progress, she felt, could so often be held back by a difference in remit as well as by cultural differences. The Early Excellence Centre bid had provided a good opportunity for people from different departments to work together and this had resulted in the formation of valuable working relationships not just within the Partnership but also across the local authority.

The Education Officer for Early Years and Childcare felt well supported by her immediate colleagues: '*People are responsive to what I'm trying to do. I have a sympathetic line manager and Partnership Chair... I feel they fully understand and support the issues that we need to address in integrating care and education.*' She has also found it helpful to network with officers in neighbouring authorities who are working on similar issues. (For example, she recently attended a conference about Bradford's new under-eights service.)

In the long term, a move towards a more integrated service could be contemplated. The perceived advantages of an integrated service would include a more efficient service and a single point of contact for parents wanting information about a range of issues, such as health, education, or benefits. The Assistant Chief Education Officer acknowledged the benefits of the integration of services for younger children: '*Unless you have a single children's services department, then it is inevitable that some things are not going to be coordinated properly.*' However, he also had concerns about the needs of older children: '*If you have a single department for younger children, you still have to interface with services for older children, so there isn't a perfect solution.*'

SUMMARY

♦ Wakefield is a metropolitan authority with a Labour-controlled council.

♦ The council has recently adopted a cabinet style of policy-making.

♦ The authority has a coordinated approach to the delivery of early childhood services. There is a dedicated early years service located in the Education Department and the authority has an independent information service for parents.

♦ The EYCDP has representatives from the authority and from private, voluntary and local authority providers.

♦ There is a need to involve officers from all departments in more joint working.

♦ The Education Officer for Early Years and Childcare feels well supported by the Partnership Chair and by her immediate line manager. She has taken a key role in contributing to the authority's bids for central government initiatives for early years and childcare.

♦ Interviewees felt that the coordination of Wakefield's early years services had led to greater efficiency and better targeting on areas of greatest need. They acknowledged that there was still work to be done on improving communication between departments and were willing to contemplate a move towards greater integration in the longer-term.

Wakefield Metropolitan Borough – *Structure for Early Years and Childcare Service*

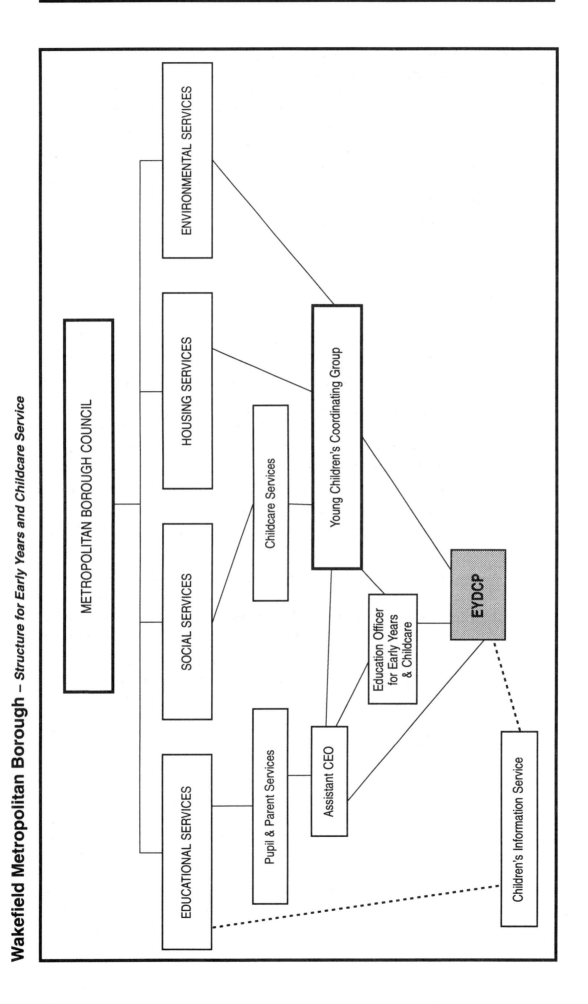

Southlea Authority

Introduction

Southlea authority is a Conservative-controlled borough. The authority has informal collaborative arrangements in place for the delivery of early education and childcare services, with officers from separate departments responsible for discrete areas of the service. Southlea is in the process of moving towards a more coordinated structure, with an Early Years Development and Childcare Unit, located in the Education Department, responsible for service delivery. There will be separate arrangements for registration and inspection in the Social Services Department.

About the local authority

Southlea is situated in the south of England. There is a recognised north–south divide in the borough, where northern areas experience high levels of unemployment, single parenthood and overcrowding, while the southern areas are relatively affluent. The northern wards also have the highest proportion of ethnic minority groups found in the borough, comprising Indian, Chinese, Black African and Black Caribbean families. Despite higher levels of socio-economic deprivation in the north, the overall unemployment figure is low (around three per cent). Employed parents are typically in clerical, mechanical and skilled manual occupations. A large number of parents are able to work outside the borough because of good transport links to other areas where there are greater employment opportunities.

The north–south divide is reflected in the nature of the available early education and childcare provision. There tend to be lower parental expectations for children's academic attainment in the northern wards and, therefore, the provision there has an emphasis on entire families, not just on children. In the southern wards, the focus tends to be on providing practical care and stimulating environments for the children of working parents.

The borough is eligible for a number of national initiatives such as Single Regeneration Budget and New Deal.

Early years provision

The authority has 540 childminders, 59 local authority nursery and reception classes, 47 private providers, three voluntary playgroups, and two independent schools which include pre-school provision.

The local capacity falls short of demand in relation to the number of childcare places available, both in particular types of provision and in certain geographical areas. When surveyed, parents felt current provision was too expensive in northern wards and not extensive enough for parents working outside the borough. There was an identified need for more provision to allow mothers to return to work.

How the structure evolved

The council operates within a traditional departmental committee structure. Directors of individual departments report directly to separate council committees. Departmental management teams ensure that individual departments are working cohesively and the Management Board of Chief Executives and Directors provides the overall coordination of corporate issues.

Southlea is an authority where the individual departments have typically worked in isolation from each other. The council was perceived to be traditional in its approach to policy and planning. Several interviewees suggested that the authority's structure had prevented a global overview and hence there was a general lack of awareness of the implications of one department's actions upon that of others. In the light of the heightened national profile of early education and childcare services, restructuring was needed to address the new policy imperatives.

The ethos of working along clear lines of departmental demarcation had made the implementation of national early years initiatives problematic for some officers. These problems had now been recognised and the necessary moves towards more 'joined-up' working were beginning to be developed within the authority at the time of the NFER visit.

Some officers from both departments felt that the rate of change, in terms of further coordination, was occurring at a faster pace within the Education Department than within Social Services. This was thought to be largely the result of the national demand for an EYDCP, led and funded by the DfEE, and the appointment of staff to facilitate change.

How the service operates

So far, Southlea has approached the delivery of early education and childcare services in a collaborative way, whereby officers from separate departments have responsibility for discrete areas of the service. Within the Education and Leisure Services Department, there are a number of early years specialists and advisers who have well-established informal working relationships with officers from across the Education Department. The specialists and advisers have also had close, yet informal, working relationships with the team of Under Eights Workers in the Social Services Department. This team has traditionally dealt with registration and inspection, and provided advice and training to providers. It also has responsibility for responding to requests for information to childcare providers.

In response to the National Childcare Strategy, the council appointed key personnel to head up an Early Years Development and Childcare Unit and to service the Partnership. These personnel included an Assistant Chief Education Officer (ACEO) on secondment from the DfEE, and an Early Years Officer with experience of working in a Social Services Department in a neighbouring authority. Both felt they were able to consider the authority from a fresh, objective perspective, which enabled them to identify weaknesses and suggest solutions to meet the new demands for service delivery. Given that the Head of Unit had been appointed from outside the authority, it was felt important to ensure the Unit would be viewed in a favourable light – by both authority officers and local providers – before changes were made. The Unit was not yet fully operational at the time of the research.

The new EYDC Unit is part of the Planning and Information Division of the Education and Leisure Services Department (see diagram). It is made up of a team of specialist early years and childcare officers and operates in response to the EYDCP. There are a number of development workers in the Unit who cater for specific groups of providers including childminders, voluntary playgroups and private and maintained providers.

It was hoped that the Unit and the Under Eights team (located in Social Services) would work closely together, given the overlap in their expertise and responsibilities. However, several of the tasks previously covered by the under-eights workers (including the Children's Information Service, training and advice) will now fall within the remit of the Unit.

The Early Years Officer acknowledged that there were cultural divisions between departments. By implementing structural changes in stages, she hoped to address these feelings of vulnerability: '*People have been doing things in the same way for many years and change is very difficult for people to accept... It is going to be a very slow process... It is about taking small steps, gradually getting people's trust.*'

The Unit is intending to increase the quality and range of provision through strategic planning. Despite an array of successful early years projects instigated by the local authority, a number of officers spoke of a history of poor communication between and within departments which they felt had led to duplication and short-term thinking. The Early Years Officer was keen to hold back from implementing policy and beginning a programme of expansion until staff were fully aware of all existing work in progress and had identified gaps in provision. She felt this could be achieved by working more closely with providers. As she suggested: '*It's more about an empowering and enabling role, rather than Unit officers coming in and doing... We need to be working alongside providers to develop and suit the cultures of those different organisations.*'

The disparate early years activities which operate in isolation from each other within different local authority departments are mirrored at service delivery level. Many of the schemes and projects set up within the community by providers lack strategic planning and hence often result in the duplication of some types of provision and the absence of others. The EYDCP has gone some way towards improving communication and coordination of local authority services.

The Partnership is chaired by a parent representative. Her status was regarded by the Unit and the Partnership as having great significance. Her independence from the Education Department and from the council members was thought to symbolise her impartiality and objectivity. In addition to her work with the Partnership, she represents parents on a wide range of committees and working groups both locally and nationally. She is vice chairperson of the Southlea Federation of Parent Teacher Associations. The fact that she represents the views of parents was felt to have ensured an end user perspective to her guidance of the Partnership.

Providers in Southlea have historically dealt with the local authority through the Social Services Department. The structural changes which will enable the Education Department to take a lead on early childhood issues will, therefore, require some explanation to providers. One private sector provider described the ambiguous status that the Education Department currently has among a number of local providers: '*Involvement of Education is a new concept for a number of private and voluntary providers… They are uncertain what role the EYDCP fulfils or what function Education plays in supporting them to deliver and plan provision*'.

However, the Partnership has assisted the Early Years Officer (EYO) and the Unit in identifying providers' needs. The Unit now plans to respond to those needs in a focused and strategic way. For example, the Unit will work to satisfy the identified need for more extensive training through the allocated childcare budget.

Although the Unit was not fully operational at the time of the research, a carefully prepared strategic plan for its inception was well developed. The ultimate intention was to have '*a streamlined seamless service*'. By working closely with the Under Eights Coordinator in Social Services, the Unit has instigated new ways of working and had improved formal coordination. But, by their own admission the ACEO and Early Years Officer agreed that: '*Coordination of services is likely to take a considerable time as it is coming from the bottom (operational staff and middle management) up.*'

Impact of the structure on policy and practice

While Southlea had collaborative arrangements in place for the delivery of its early education and childcare services, change was still ongoing at the time of the NFER research. The officers interviewed were, however, optimistic about the impact that the Early Years Development and Childcare Unit was likely to have in the future.

The admittedly slow rate of change to date had been influenced by two main factors: the political persuasion of the council and the traditional working practices within the local authority. The Conservative-controlled council, unsurprisingly, had different priorities to those of a Labour central government. This presented certain problems for officers seeking to implement national initiatives.

The more significant inhibiting factor was thought to be the traditional working practices and entrenched beliefs within the local authority. The long-established structure of the authority, with defined departmental boundaries coupled with a general resistance to change among some senior officers, was perceived to present the greatest obstacle to moving towards 'joined-up' working. Many officers had had long careers within the local authority and it was felt they did not welcome structural change. As one officer commented: '*People in Southlea don't generally work well together. Turf war would be putting it too strongly, but there is quite a strong concern about responsibilities, as to where they stop and start.*'

Historically, informal liaison among officers had provided the platform for cross-departmental working. However, such *ad hoc* arrangements were criticised for being dependent on individual personalities and therefore unreliable. In order to put the National Childcare Strategy into operation and achieve 'joined-up' working, certain officers recognised the need for more formalised communication and greater coordination.

The introduction of the National Childcare Strategy in 1998 had acted as the impetus for initial restructuring in the local authority. Early education and childcare services fell within the remit of the Education Department because of the budgetary allocation – a situation which necessitated the reallocation of responsibility from the Under Eights Team to a new Unit of early years specialists within the Education Department. The reluctance by many long-serving officers to change their working practices (prompted in part by feelings of uncertainty about their job remit) meant that such change had to be approached cautiously.

The new policy imperative was a major driving force behind the setting up of the new Unit, as the ACEO suggested: '*Officers and local providers are more likely to accept the changes proposed by the Unit because they have been set out by central government through the National Childcare Strategy. If the call for change had not come from government and been directly funded, it would probably have been dismissed out of hand as there is benevolent complacency that the present situation works and therefore there is no need for change.*'

The appointment of external personnel to manage the Early Years Development and Childcare Unit has also had significant implications for the nature and rate of change. The ACEO has taken a proactive role in the work of the EYDCP and the new Unit. Through effective liaison, he had taken the views of the officers, Partnership members and local providers to the council members through the Education Management Group. By relaying messages back and forth between practitioners and council, the basis for more effective communication had been established.

The Early Years Officer had also played a central role in terms of instigating more coordinated planning and service delivery. She faced a series of obstacles in the initial stages. As a newcomer to the authority, it had taken time for her to familiarise herself with the authority, as she described: '*When I came into post as a non-Southlea person, things were difficult because it has taken me a long while to discover who is doing what and where, and then to work out how that fits in with the Unit... A lot of people in Southlea have been here a long time... If you're not part of that set-up, it makes it quite difficult because people take for granted that you should know what they know... It is that sort of arrangement... It has taken me quite a while to realise everything is quite uncoordinated.*'

At the time of the research, the familiarisation stage was complete and the Unit was about to embark on putting strategic plans into operation. Needs had been identified through the work of the Partnership and the auditing of parental views about early education and childcare had begun. The Unit was planning to begin an expansion and development programme on the basis of this information. However, it had taken a considerable time to collate relevant information and set up systems for more coordination, both inside and outside of the local authority. The Unit was still faced with the task of raising its profile with officers, providers and parents. As the EYO acknowledged: '*People have been saying "We didn't even know you were there." We have to have a much higher profile, both in the authority and among providers and parents... I want to be able to give a really positive message that we are able to support people in all areas of early education and childcare.*'

The foundations for greater coordination had begun to be established and the Unit staff were optimistic about the future and the benefits to providers, parents and children. The EYO felt that greater coordination and strategic direction would provide the community with a better service: '*To have coordinated services will benefit families... If the Unit knows what is going on in the community, even if it is still fragmented, we will have an overview of everything that is happening. If we pull together, we can provide better-quality services and get people involved and reflect on the standards, vulnerability of children, the impact on people and the needs of parents. It is about widening it up and having the resources to deliver much more. It doesn't matter who is delivering it as long as it is coordinated.*'

SUMMARY

- Southlea is a borough in the south of England with a Conservative-controlled council.

- The authority has a well-established organisational structure, with clearly defined departmental boundaries, cultures and traditional working practices.

- There is a shortfall of early education and childcare provision – both in the number of places available and the range of settings – to satisfy parental need.

- Southlea is currently using a collaborative approach to early years provision, where officers in separate departments had responsibility for discrete areas of the service. However, the authority is planning to move towards greater coordination of services.

- The increased national emphasis on 'joined-up' working was providing the impetus for change within and between departments.

- The process of change was being carefully planned and implemented by two officers, both of whom were appointed from outside the authority. Their previous professional experiences were felt to be important in terms of facilitating change.

- The officers spent a considerable time familiarising themselves with existing working patterns and service delivery to ensure strategic changes were made.

- The officers established an Early Years Development and Childcare Unit to deliver the service. Until that time, it had been delivered through a series of *ad hoc* working arrangements between officers from across the authority.

- Although the Unit was not yet fully operational at the time of the research, interviewees were optimistic that it would bring greater coordination to the planning and delivery of the early years service.

Southlea Local Authority – *Structure for Early Years and Childcare Service*

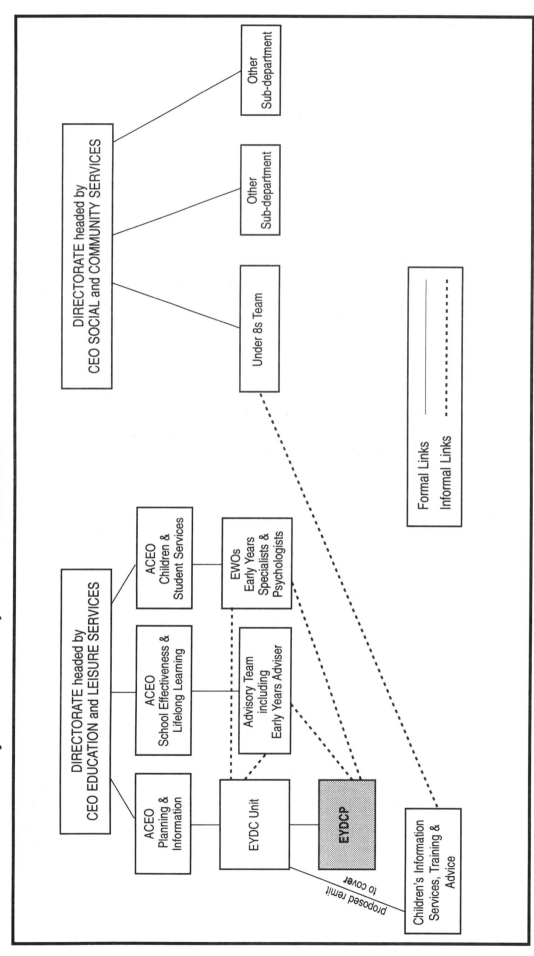

Fulsham Authority

Introduction

Fulsham is a Conservative-controlled authority that has collaborative arrangements in place for the delivery of early education and childcare services. An Early Years Officer, based in the Education Department, has responsibility for the service and liaises with the EYDCP. A body of elected representatives and senior officers from the Education and Cultural Services Committee oversees the service.

About the local authority

Fulsham became a unitary authority in 1998. Previously, it was one of several districts within a county council. Fulsham is one of the largest of the newly formed authorities.

The vast majority (97 per cent) of families who live in the authority are from White European backgrounds. Fulsham and its surrounding areas have a very low index of socio-economic deprivation: there is very little unemployment (around one per cent) or single parenthood (approximately two per cent). The local economy relies primarily on service industries, including the retail, banking, finance and communication sectors. White collar professional families, typically with two children, live in the area. It is still common for mothers not to work outside the home.

As one of the least deprived authorities in England, Fulsham does not qualify for national regeneration and social inclusion initiatives, such as Sure Start.

Early years provision

The authority has 555 registered providers of early years education and childcare, including 440 childminders, 44 voluntary pre-schools and playgroups, 41 local authority schools which have reception and or nursery classes, 12 private day nurseries, 12 private nursery schools and six independent schools.

The supply of childcare broadly matches parental demand. There are few LEA-funded four-year-old places in Fulsham, which has resulted in parents opting for voluntary or private provision. Accessibility to provision is considered to be unproblematic for most families given the sound infrastructure, working patterns and relative affluence of most families living in the area. The authority had DfEE funding for 37 places for three-year-olds in 1999–2000. Children aged three are admitted to spare places in nursery classes when all four-year-olds have been admitted.

How the structure evolved

Fulsham has developed an organisational structure based on the working practices that were already in operation in the former county council. Since gaining unitary status, the authority has become more focused on its own local policy and delivery of services.

The pattern of existing early education and childcare provision has, to some extent, determined the structure of the Early Years Service within the local authority. The voluntary and private sectors are the largest providers and, as such, the local authority has adopted a detached approach to managing the Early Years Service. Early education and childcare services feature as a relatively low priority in terms of local authority policy.

Elected representatives work within a committee structure. There is a separate committee for Education and Cultural Services and another for Community Services. Councillors typically chair the departmental committees and sit on a series of working groups, including the Children's Services Working Group. The political composition of the council plus the presence of elected members on the range of working groups were perceived, by a number of our interviewees, to have created certain tensions in implementing central government initiatives at local level.

As a unitary authority in its infancy, Fulsham's structure is still evolving. The statutory requirement to convene an Early Years Development and Childcare Partnership led to the appointment of a dedicated local authority officer in 1998 to act as the coordinator for all matters relating to the Partnership. At the time of the NFER study in 1999, a number of new officers were being appointed and the Education Department was awaiting the appointment of a new Director. The officers interviewed felt the influx of new personnel and the constant structural changes created barriers to developing a clear strategic direction.

When the research was carried out, the Early Years Service was based in the Education and Cultural Services Department. Within this department, there are four main sub divisions: Quality and School Support, Pupil Support, School Provision and Access, and Cultural Services and Lifelong Learning. Initially, the Early Years Service was attached to the Pupil Support division (see diagram). Pupil Support included a team of Educational Psychologists, SEN experts, Education Welfare Officers and officers concerned with the integration of pupil support services. However, there were plans in place (at the time of the NFER research) to relocate the Early Years Service in the School Provision and Access strand (see postscript).

The Early Years Officer runs the service and liaises with officers in Educational and Cultural Services and Community Services on an *ad hoc* basis, usually for purposes of information exchange.

How the service operates

The Early Years Service is run solely by the Early Years Officer (EYO), who is a former nursery head from a maintained school outside the authority. As the post is relatively new and its associated roles and responsibilities are unfamiliar to other officers, she is required to instigate intra- and inter-departmental working relationships that had not previously existed.

Servicing the Partnership has provided the officer with the focus and motivation needed to meet statutory requirements and develop relationships among officers and providers. However, further coordination of services lies outside her remit. There are no structures or plans, other than the EYDCP Plan, to facilitate coordination, either internally or externally.

The Under Eights Team of advisers is based in the Community Services Department. The majority of them are employed on a part-time basis and their remit – in terms of early education and childcare – is focused on the care aspect. The team has minimal contact with officers outside Community Services, although the appointment of the Early Years Officer has called for some degree of collaboration. Most of the contact between the team and the Early Years Officer has been around the exchange of information required for the EYDCP Plan.

The Early Years Officer's main duties and responsibilities, as set out in her job description, include: developing quality in all early years provision; establishing policy and practice; arranging, delivering and participating in training opportunities for providers; maintaining a watching brief on relevant research and best working practices in early years; preparing funding bids to support development; and ensuring effective liaison with schools, other education services, Community Services, Health and other statutory and voluntary agencies.

The officer felt that her heavy administrative workload had encroached on her ability to satisfy the broader objectives associated with the Early Years Service, but she felt able to fulfil the short-term objectives through the Partnership.

The Early Years Officer had taken the lead in developing the Early Years Childcare and Development Plan, which included a number of tasks ranging from a childcare audit to surveying parental views and collating information from different departments to establish the nature, extent and quality of early years provision available to parents in Fulsham. From the Plan, a series of objectives were identified which were to be met via the Partnership. A number of interviewees felt the Partnership had provided the major platform upon which officers, from within and across departments, were able to operate in a coordinated way.

The full Partnership is made up of all the requisite representatives (apart from an employer). The composition of provider representatives is skewed in favour of the voluntary and private sectors, reflecting the pattern of provision in the area. The Partnership includes officers from Community Services, Health Services and Education and Cultural Services. A small number of task groups stem from the full Partnership to achieve the identified objectives. These task groups include: Access and Special Educational Needs (SEN); New Childcare Places; Recruitment, Training and Quality Provision; and Information. Each task group comprises approximately six members, some of whom are local authority officers.

The remits for each task group are centred on making adjustments to pre-existing structures and services. For example, the brief for the Access and SEN task group is focused on improving training for providers to identify children's special needs at the earliest possible time. Other considerations, such as access for minority groups, are relatively unproblematic given the very small proportion of such groups in the area. Similarly, access to information is already well established in the area so the task group has taken on responsibility for improving the existing dissemination strategy.

The work for the other task groups is equally focused. The New Childcare Places group, for example, is able to concentrate on out-of-school provision and holiday clubs because the supply of early years provision meets parental demand and projected figures suggest that the population of under-fives is likely to remain static.

Given that there is sufficient quality training available, the Recruitment, Training and Quality Task Group's purpose is to plan a dissemination strategy to ensure that all providers are aware of the training available through the local authority. The Early Years Officer is specifically responsible for providing advice and support concerning training and recruitment to providers and potential providers.

An established Children's Information Centre (situated in a neighbouring authority) meets the statutory requirements for comprehensive and accessible information on early education and childcare services for parents and providers. Therefore, the Information Task Group has been assigned responsibility for establishing a satellite service based in Fulsham to ensure access to more localised information.

Impact of the structure on policy and practice

Those interviewed in Fulsham were local authority officers and early years representatives. Senior Officers and elected representatives declined the invitation to participate. However, the participants represented a range of views about the purpose and effectiveness of the Early Years Service in Fulsham.

Several factors were felt to have determined the shape and nature of the Early Years Service in the authority. These included: central government statutory requirements; the Conservative council; Fulsham's new unitary status and its evolving organisational structure; the relative affluence within the authority; and the extensive existing private and voluntary provision.

Because Fulsham has a Conservative-controlled council, its priorities differ from the objectives of the Labour Government. As a result, the Early Years Service was given a relatively low status on the local government agenda. This was reinforced when the councillors approved the EYDCP Plan in 1999, but placed a disclaimer on it disassociating the council from the Partnership: '*The views in the plan were those of the Partnership and did not in any way reflect the position of the council.*'

In common with other authorities where the Early Years Service was the responsibility of a single person, the professional isolation of the Early Years Officer was a potential problem. The Early Years Officer felt her role was misunderstood by many officers both within and across departments. Since her appointment, she had been given responsibility for many tasks outside her remit which had taken time and attention away from other priorities. This has been compounded by the changes in location of the Service and the considerable administrative workload associated with servicing the Partnership. As one early years provider commented: '*There is only one Early Years Officer... who is fighting our cause... With her workload there is only so much one person can do*'.

The pattern of early education and childcare provision within the authority was felt to have a significant impact upon the scope and purpose of the local authority Early Years Service. Provision is primarily available from the private and voluntary sectors, which have traditionally worked in isolation from each other. Apart from limited contact with the local authority, for purposes of registration and inspection or training, both sectors are largely self-sufficient.

The voluntary and private sectors were initially hostile to the appointment of the Early Years Officer. One private provider confided that the EYO post had been perceived as the '*repressive arm of the local authority*' upon their provision and their preferred ways of working. However, over time, and through the Partnership, providers had come to regard the Early Years Officer as a reliable source of support and advice. They had welcomed the Partnership as an opportunity to share practice and to streamline the range of provision on offer in Fulsham. As one private provider commented: '*The Partnership has been helpful because I have met a range of people involved with the early years including paediatricians... The personal contacts that you make have helped establish further links with the maintained sector... It has helped me to understand what the Early Years Service is for.*'

The EYDCP was thought to have a low profile among elected representatives and senior officers, despite the fact that it was the main mechanism by which the officers from different departments coordinated their work on early years. Providers were critical of the lack of coordination between departments within the local authority: '*At the moment there is a lack of unity, and the information providers get from one department is totally different from another… It is very difficult to work with different departments when everybody seems to think differently.'*

The Early Years Officer and those Partnership members interviewed felt that both the working relationships in Fulsham and the status of the Partnership could benefit from greater coordination. One provider reinforced these views: *'Further coordination in the form of employing more people within the local authority would show the value and importance of the early years to people in Fulsham. It would stop duplication… People could move forward, overcome conflict, try to resolve issues… If local authority people worked together, time would not be wasted.'* Nevertheless, the Early Years Officer felt the current early education and childcare service was operating as well as possible given the lack of coordination. She explained: *'I look after the providers as best I can and keep them as informed as I can… The training and development programme is as good as I can do. I think they are well supported.'*

Postscript

Since the NFER research was completed, a new Director of Education has been appointed in Fulsham. The restructuring proposed by his predecessor has been reversed and the Early Years Service remains within the Pupil Support Division of the Directorate.

SUMMARY

♦ Fulsham is a new authority and has a Conservative-controlled council.

♦ The priorities of the councillors tend to differ markedly from those of the Labour Government.

♦ The authority has collaborative arrangements in place for the delivery of early education and childcare services. The main providers are in the voluntary and private sectors.

♦ Early education and childcare services have a relatively low priority in terms of local authority policy.

♦ The Early Years Service is delivered through the EYDCP by the Early Years Officer, who has sole responsibility for the service. Her role is to service the Partnership and coordinate all early years matters within the authority. As she is alone, there are potential problems of professional isolation from colleagues both in the Education and the Social Services Departments.

♦ The EYDCP is the main platform on which collaboration occurs, both among local authority officers and early years providers. Through the Partnership, the Early Years Service objectives are met.

♦ Interviewees felt greater coordination was needed to ensure more effective working relationships between officers and a higher status for the Early Years Service among elected representatives.

Fulsham Local Authority – *Structure for Early Years and Childcare Service*

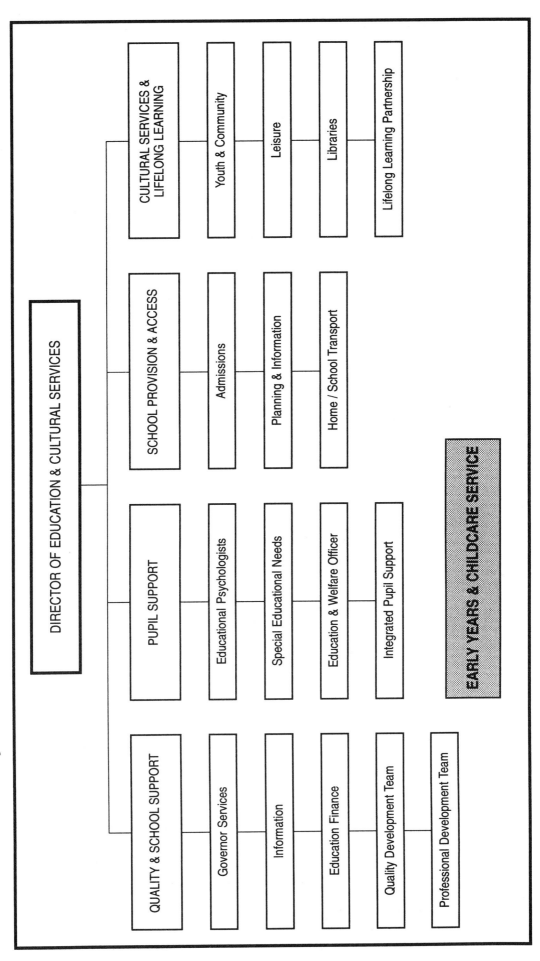

DIRECTOR OF EDUCATION & CULTURAL SERVICES

QUALITY & SCHOOL SUPPORT
- Governor Services
- Information
- Education Finance
- Quality Development Team
- Professional Development Team

PUPIL SUPPORT
- Educational Psychologists
- Special Educational Needs
- Education & Welfare Officer
- Integrated Pupil Support

SCHOOL PROVISION & ACCESS
- Admissions
- Planning & Information
- Home / School Transport

CULTURAL SERVICES & LIFELONG LEARNING
- Youth & Community
- Leisure
- Libraries
- Lifelong Learning Partnership

EARLY YEARS & CHILDCARE SERVICE

REFERENCES

AUDIT COMMISSION (1996). *Counting to Five*. London: HMSO.

AUDIT COMMISSION (1997). *Counting to Five: a Review of Audits of Education for Under-fives*. London: Audit Commission.

EISENSTADT, N. (1999). 'Implementing Sure Start', *Education Journal*, **33**, 5.

GREAT BRITAIN. DEPARTMENT FOR EDUCATION AND EMPLOYMENT (1998). *Meeting the Childcare Challenge: a Framework and Consultation Document* (Cm.3959). London: The Stationery Office.

GREAT BRITAIN. DEPARTMENT FOR EDUCATION AND EMPLOYMENT (1999a). *Sixty Six Thousand New Childcare Places – Hodge Exceeds Target* (DfEE News 273/99). London: DfEE.

GREAT BRITAIN. DEPARTMENT FOR EDUCATION AND EMPLOYMENT (1999b). *Early Years Development and Childcare Partnership: Planning Guidance 2000-2001*. London: DfEE.

GREAT BRITAIN. PARLIAMENT. HOUSE OF COMMONS (1972). *Education: a Framework for Expansion* (Cmnd.5174). London: HMSO.

GREAT BRITAIN. PARLIAMENT. HOUSE OF COMMONS (1999). *Modernising Government* (Cm.4310). London: The Stationery Office.

GREAT BRITAIN. STATUTES (1989). *Children Act 1989. Chapter 41*. London: HMSO.

GREAT BRITAIN. STATUTES (1990). *National Health Service and Community Care Act 1990. Chapter 19*. London: HMSO.

JAMIESON, A. and OWEN, S. (2000). *Ambition for Change: Partnerships, Children and Work*. London: National Children's Bureau.

LOCAL GOVERNMENT ASSOCIATION (1998). *Sure Start Initiative* (Circular 615/98). London: LGA.

McQUAIL, S. and PUGH, G. (1995). *Effective Organisation of Early Childhood Services*. London: National Children's Bureau.

OWEN, S. (1995). 'The limits of co-ordination as a strategy', *International Journal of Educational Management* (Special Edition: *Nursery Education*), **9**, 3, 19-22.

APPENDICES

Appendix 1: Proforma sent to all local authorities

NFER RESEARCH
Developing Early Education and Childcare Services

Please tick the appropriate box

A) *Essentially a single department/service* *

- We have joint working arrangements/structures for under fives (comprising Education and other services) that meet as a single body.
- We have a single management line, with the head of the services for under fives reporting to a service department (e.g. education).
- We have budgetary control for most services for under fives.

☐

B) *Essentially separate departments/services* which collaborate within a formal structure.*

- We have separate working arrangements/structures for the main under fives services.
- We have some joint working arrangements/structures, which report back to the main services.
- We have a separate management line for social services and education, but there are formal arrangements for co-ordination (e.g. post of responsibility for early years).

☐

C) *Essentially separate departments/services**

- We have no joint arrangements for under fives services.
- We have separate management lines in social services and education.
- We have few formal arrangements for co-ordination.

☐

COMMENTS ....

....

....

*Notes Services for under fives may be part of a wider brief e.g. for children aged under eight.
These definitions are based on previous research conducted by the National Children's Bureau (McQuail, S. and Pugh, G. 1995. *Effective Organisation of Early Childhood Services*. London: National Children's Bureau).

PLEASE RETURN THIS FORM TO JAYNE OSGOOD AT NFER, USING THE ENVELOPE PROVIDED. THANK YOU.

Appendix 2

Members of the Advisory Group

Julia Bennett (and later) Kirsten Liddell
Lead Officer for Early Years
Local Government Association (LGA)

David Bruce
Lead Officer for Early Years
Luton Borough Council

Marilyn Cohen
Early Years Development Officer
London Borough of Hammersmith & Fulham

Margaret Lochrie
Chief Executive
Pre-school Learning Alliance (PLA)

Sue Owen
Principal Officer, Early Childhood Unit
National Children's Bureau (NCB)